GOD

THAN WE CAN IMAGINE

GOD IS ALWAYS BETTER THAN WE CAN IMAGINE

Thirty-one Meditations on the Greatness of God

Iain Wright

To Becky
With love
Grandma Boss
2019

THE BANNER OF TRUTH TRUST

THE BANNER OF TRUTH TRUST

Head Office
3 Murrayfield Road
Edinburgh
EH12 6EL
UK

North America Office
PO Box 621
Carlisle
PA 17013
USA

banneroftruth.org

© Iain Wright 2019

*

ISBN
Print: 978 1 84871 934 7
EPUB: 978 1 84871 935 4
Kindle: 978 1 84871 936 1

*

Typeset in 10/14 Sabon Oldstyle
at The Banner of Truth Trust, Edinburgh

Printed in the USA by
Versa Press Inc.,
East Peoria, IL.

For the Saints at Covenant
who are never far from my thoughts
and always in my affections

Contents

Foreword

I do not usually find most present-day devotional material all that helpful, not the way Spurgeon's well-known *Morning and Evening* has been (and still is). But now and then there is an exception. And this fine effort by my good friend Iain Wright is such an exception. Right away as I began reading these devotionals it struck me that they are much like Spurgeon's, and that for one simple reason: Iain (like Spurgeon) has a mind and heart saturated with the whole content of Scripture. Because of this, wherever he takes us in the Bible, we are always helped to see a particular part in the light of the whole plan of redemption.

Another thing that must be said about these devotionals is this—and it may be the most important—Iain interacts with the Scriptures in the same way that Spurgeon did: he quite simply believes them. If God says he made the earth in six days, that is simply believed by Iain. That is the reason why these devotionals are wonderfully free from any sense of contemporary uncertainty about what is true and right and what is false and wrong. God's word is Iain's only rule of faith and practice. This is the same great principle that guided the Westminster divines who gave us the Confession of Faith and the Larger and Shorter Catechisms.[1] Not surprisingly the same truths expounded in those documents pervade these devotionals.

The third thing that has impressed itself on me in reading Iain's short chapters is the note of optimism they convey. We are living at a time when every single day seems to bring another event that is truly depressing. There is no answer to this except to come to see how great God is and to understand his plan for the future of the cosmos. This, too, is always present in these thirty-one devotional meditations.

May it please God to use this book to encourage and strengthen his elect people in the faith that can never be defeated.

G. I. WILLIAMSON
Sheldon, Iowa

[1] These important and historic teaching documents can be found in *The Confession of Faith* (Edinburgh: Banner of Truth Trust, 2018).

Meditation 1

O, Magnify the Lord with Me!

For this reason I bow my knees before the Father, from whom every family in heaven and on earth is named, that according to the riches of his glory he may grant you to be strengthened with power through his Spirit in your inner being, so that Christ may dwell in your hearts through faith— that you, being rooted and grounded in love, may have strength to comprehend with all the saints what is the breadth and length and height and depth, and to know the love of Christ that surpasses knowledge, that you may be filled with all the fullness of God. Now to him who is able to do far more abundantly than all that we ask or think, according to the power at work within us, to him be glory in the church and in Christ Jesus throughout all generations, forever and ever. Amen.—Ephesians 3:14-21.

Everyone has a 'theology.' Your neighbour who never goes to church has a theology. The atheist who takes every opportunity to mock Christianity has a theology. And you have one too. By theology, I mean there are certain things we are able to say about God; believe about him, and the manner in which we interact with him.

Though this will annoy the God-hating atheist, he too has a theology. He will not acknowledge it, but he is 'suppressing the truth in unrighteousness' (cf. Rom. 1:18). Your neighbour who never goes to church also has a theology. He probably doesn't deny that there is a god. He may even have some loosely Christian notions of who God is and can list some of his 'attributes'. Even as he does so, he sets God at a distance while he gets on with his own life. For him, tragically, God is a bit like the President of the United States. Sure he's important, but for more than a third of the electorate, voting at election time is so low a priority that they just don't do it. The President is far away, and getting on with life is more important to them. Isn't that how most folk think of God?

So right at the beginning, let me challenge you by asking, 'What do you think of God? What is *your* theology?'

David, the Old Testament writer of many of the Psalms, encourages his readers in Psalm 34:3: 'Oh, magnify the LORD with me!' What exactly is he telling his readers to do? Can we somehow make God bigger? I hope your theology is better than that! We cannot enlarge the attributes of an infinite and eternal God. How then can we 'magnify the Lord'? Perhaps an illustration may help. I expect most parents have shown a child some tiny object, perhaps a leaf or a bug, and brought out the magnifying glass. 'Here, look at this!' Under the magnifying glass the object appears much larger and we see it more clearly. That surely helps us to understand something of what the Psalmist means. As we look more closely at what God has revealed about himself we will see him more clearly and learn more about him.

The meditations in this little book follow David's counsel in Psalm 34. They will encourage you to magnify the Lord with me. But I have also written them with a particular application in mind.

Turn with me to another part of the Bible, to Exodus 33, which records a conversation that Moses had with the Lord. It took place at an unhappy time in the history of God's people. The Lord had delivered his people out of Egypt, out of the 'house of bondage.' He had called Moses to meet with him on top of a mountain. While the Lord was in the very process of giving Moses the Ten Commandments, down in the valley below the children of Israel 'sat down to eat and drink and rose up to play' (verse 6). It is in the aftermath of that sorry day in Israel's history, that Moses opens his heart out to God. His first request is stated simply: 'please show me now your ways, that I may know you' (verse 13).

His request is most interesting, for it reveals Moses' desire to have a 'theology' or knowledge of God that does not come from his own thinking and which is not the product of his own imagination. If he is to know God, then God must show him his ways. Moses wants to know God really and truly. He therefore asks God to reveal himself: 'show me your ways.' It is through God's ways that Moses will know God.

3

Isn't that how God still deals with us? We only come to know him through his gracious dealings with us. Perhaps the greatest theologian of all time, the apostle Paul, expressed this well when he spoke of how he had come to know God. God had not only called him by his grace but had also 'revealed his Son' to him (see Gal. 1:15-16). God had shown him 'his ways.'

Returning to Exodus 33, the Lord informs Moses that he must lead the people to the Promised Land but that the Lord would not go with them. That message sent a chill down Moses' spine: 'If your Presence does not go with us, do not send us up from here!' What do these words reveal about Moses? They open a window into his soul and show us something of the love that burned in his heart for the Lord. He cannot bear the thought of being parted from the Lord's presence. Is that not also true of all who have come to know God's ways and who love him in return? Those who love the Lord will never want to be separated from him. We want to be near the one we love (cf. Psa. 73:25-26, 28; 65:4).

But notice another aspect of this relationship with the Lord that Moses also brings out: 'If your Presence does not go with us ... what else will distinguish me and your people from all the other people on the face of the earth?' (Exod. 33:15-16). The distinguishing feature of God's people is that he is with them! A child of God is marked out as one who knows God, who loves God, who lives his life in God's presence.

Perhaps in that context we can better understand

Moses' next request: 'Please show me your glory' (verse 18). Do you see the progression in Moses' thought? He wants to know God's ways, so that he might know God himself. Knowing God, he does not want to be separated from him. Walking with God, he wants to see his glory. He is not asking for wealth, long life, power, or a reputation for himself, but for God's glory! What a challenge as a model of prayer. 'Whatever else you do, Lord, show me your glory!'

It is at that point that the Lord sets Moses in the cleft of the rock—and what happens next? The Lord causes all his 'goodness' to pass in front of Moses.

Now what do you know of the goodness of God? If you are a child of God, you already know something of the riches of his goodness towards you in sending his Son to die for you. He has forgiven your sins and given you a 'joy that is inexpressible and filled with glory' (1 Pet. 1:8). But how great is this goodness of God? Our theology will determine how we answer that question.

The goodness of God is as great as the person of God: it is therefore infinite and eternal. Can you comprehend the infinite? Can you come to its end and say: 'Now I know all there is to know about the goodness of God'? No, when you think you have understood all there is to know about God's goodness, God will surprise you with still more, for *God is always better than we can imagine.*

Now here is how Paul deals with this theme. He wrote to the church in Ephesus to encourage them in the gospel. At roughly the midpoint in his letter he breaks out into a doxology—he wanted to praise God's glory and he did so by pointing to God's goodness. I can picture him bent over his desk scribbling out the words,

'Now to him who is able to do what we ask, to him be glory in the church.'

That's true, but it is not nearly good enough; so he takes up his pen again:

'Now to him who is able to do *all* that we ask, to him be glory in the church.'

Then he takes up his pen again for what has been written is not quite sufficient to express fully the thought:

'Now to him who is able to do *more than* all we ask ...'

No, God can do more than that!

'Now to him who is able to do more *abundantly* than all that we ask ...'

No, that's still not quite enough!

'Now to him who is able to do *far* more abundantly than all that we ask ...'

Yes, yes, but *God is always better than we can imagine.*

'Now to him who is able to do far more abundantly above all that we ask *or think* ...'

I would urge you to take these meditations and read one each day for a month with this great biblical theme in mind. Read them to your children as part of family devotions. Ponder what the word of God teaches you and each day come to God's word with Moses' request in mind, 'Show me your ways that I may know you!'

'Oh magnify the Lord with me,' for *God is always better than you can imagine!*

For further reflection:

1. Do you know all there is to know about God?

2. How can you get to know him better?

3. What will be the consequences of knowing God better?

Meditation 2

Felix Culpa

> I will put enmity between you and the woman, and
> between your offspring and her offspring; he shall
> bruise your head, and you shall bruise his heel.
>
> —Genesis 3:15.

My English teacher's favourite play was *Oedipus Rex*. He told me once that he had read it so many times that he had long since lost count. When I asked why he had read it so often, he responded that each time he turned to it, he hoped that its story would turn out differently. I didn't understand him at the time, and so far as his particular favourite play was concerned, I still don't really share his hope. But perhaps I have come to share his wistful desire that the inevitability of a story's ending might, contrary to all logic, strangely change. I have something of that longing every time I read the opening chapters of Genesis.

I am, no doubt, biased, but would argue that I have every right to be. God sovereignly and unapologetically summons the world into being. He has but to speak the word and from nothing all is created. At the mere declaration of his will a universe is set in the place he has appointed for it. There is something unspeakably majestic about the exercise of his will. Who indeed can stay his hand or deny him his desires?

As God looks upon all the works his hands have made he pronounces his own benediction at the end of the sixth day of Creation: 'It was very good!

From the grandeur of the display of his naked power we are then brought into the intimacy of his creation of one formed in his image and placed in Eden to tend the garden. There is something quite splendidly poignant about God's assessment of Adam's position with respect to the rest of creation. Though the garden was created in perfection, as God looked upon the one who bore his image, even in his creature's unfallen purity, he declared that it was not good for him to be alone. The animals were brought before him, and he gave names to each one; but among all that vast array not one was found to be a suitable helper for him. Even in paradise, or so it would appear, there was something lacking: a helper suitable for Adam.

It is unfortunate, to say the least, that heated debates over the roles of men and women have obscured some of the beauty and some of the truth of these words and their implications. Let me illustrate a simple truth. Some years ago, I worked for a Christian charity. It was my privilege to visit a number of European cities on its behalf. On one trip I visited Stockholm, before catching the ferry to Helsinki in Finland. I had a little free time in

Helsinki and was impressed by a most striking European capital. But for all the beautiful grandeur of the city and its buildings, my real desire was to be back at home with my wife and family. I would rather have been with them in the most ordinary of surroundings, than be without them in the grandest.

Edward Fitzgerald captured something of that strange contrast in part of his translation of a thousand-year-old Persian poem:

A Book of Verses underneath the Bough,
A Jug of Wine, a Loaf of Bread—and Thou
Beside me singing in the Wilderness—
Oh, Wilderness were Paradise enow!

The presence of the one you love turns the wilderness into a paradise. Being made in the image of God means that we cannot happily exist in isolation, even if the isolation is Paradise itself.

Having brought Adam and Eve together, the greatest catastrophe in the history of the world unfolds in the third chapter of Genesis. How many times have I read the story of the fall? More times than I care to remember. And like my English teacher, though it is contrary to all logic, there is something within me that hopes that the next time I read it the story will change.

As we know, the temptation is laid before Adam and Eve, and both, catastrophically, disastrously, hideously, fall from perfection to brokenness and worse. The expectation is contrasted with the reality in just a few measured words. Our first parents heard *the voice of the Lord walking in the garden* in the cool of the day. To be sure it is a strange expression, but the voice that had summoned the world into being now comes to meet with those whom he had formed in his own image. Of course, it is impossible to be utterly detached from these words, living as we do in a world that bears testimony to the fall on every hand; but it is no less heartbreaking for all that, to have displayed to our view a God who seeks out fellowship with his creatures, and creatures who for their part hide from his presence. There is something unmistakably moving in the first question God ever asks of man, 'Where are you?' God is quite clearly not seeking to fill a gap in his knowledge, as though he were ignorant of man's physical location.

The great enemy of souls had promised a change in man's position. By taking the fruit Adam and Eve would be as gods. But had their position changed? Yes, it had. But not in the direction they had thought. From the bliss of fellowship with their Creator in Paradise, they were now reduced to hiding from him out of fear.

Following on from their sin and rebellion came the inevitable judgment. Shall not the Judge of all the earth do right? Death, the ultimate separation, entered into the world, and Adam and Eve are ejected from the Garden of Eden. But not just yet. The curse of their rebellion is laid before them. But before God has completed his pronouncement on the serpent, he made a promise that the seed of the woman will bruise the serpent's head. If

Adam and Eve had been paying strict attention, they would have heard that God was promising that the death penalty would not be inflicted immediately. The stay of execution was good news. But *God is always better than we can imagine*. Not only does God speak of one not yet born, but he promises that *that person* will come to bruise the head of the serpent.

But there is more. Animals were sacrificed there in the garden, whose skins were used to clothe our first parents. If we were to say that blood was shed to protect them from the consequences of their sin, our thinking would inevitably be drawn to the one who is ultimately our only protection against the consequences of our wayward rebellion.

But still there is more. Had we been Adam and Eve, for what might we have wished? If only the clock could be made to run in reverse. Let us have the moment over again so that the story might have a different ending. Who among us has lived any length of time and has not looked back on a day with the longing that we might be able to take back a word, or make a different decision?

And perhaps we, too, might wish that, even with the passing of so many centuries, time might be reversed and that we might even yet be living in Paradise. In a world that is so often filled with much pain, such a desire is more than understandable.

But *God is always better than we can imagine*. It is at this point that I should declare my long-felt dissatisfaction with the simple explanation often given for the meaning of the biblical term 'justified.' You may have come across it too. 'Justified means "just-as-if-I'd never sinned."' Every time I hear it I am more convinced that it is inadequate to describe what God has done for us in Christ. To break open the point let me ask this: Is God's great work of redemption to make us like Adam before the fall, or to make us like Christ after the resurrection? Every warm-hearted believer will immediately respond that we have been raised up in Christ—we are his new creation.

In giving his judgment upon our first parents in Genesis 3, streaks of gospel light shine through: unmerited blessings follow when only punishment is deserved. I might have desired that God would make me like Adam before the fall but what God promises is to make me like his Son. No wonder the Psalmist exclaims, 'when I awake, I shall be satisfied with his likeness' (Psa. 17:15).[1]

But there is still more. For *God is always better than we can imagine.*

Suppose, just for a moment, that your neighbour, a kindly man, large of heart and great of means, often tells you that he is more than willing to do whatever he can for you and for your family. His affection for you is genuine and cannot be doubted. It seems that every day he renews the offer, and he has given you many tokens of his care. Then on one catastrophic day you lose your means of providing for yourself: you return home only to find your house razed to the ground the day after

---

[1] See Meditation 23 for more on this great theme.

your insurance policy ran out. Your neighbour who has so often protested the greatness of his affection for you, now makes good his word in countless ways. You are welcomed into his home and bidden to enjoy it as if all that he has is now yours. Your own rather modest dwelling place is no more, but in its place you have the finest of mansions, and much more beside.

Well, eye has not seen nor has ear heard, indeed it has not entered into the heart of man what things God has prepared for those who love him (cf. 1 Cor 2:8).

Had we lived a thousand years in Paradise, and every day of those thousand years had been concluded with fellowship with God in the cool of the day; and on each occasion he had gently and tenderly told us of his love; would we have conceived his love for us to be so great that he would send his one and only Son to die in our place?

Gabriel and Michael and all the host of the elect angels can and do sing the praise of his wondrous glory. But it is only broken sinners alone in this universe who are able to sing of his redeeming love. We shall not lightly surrender so high a privilege.

For further reflection:

1. Does God redeem you to make you like Adam before the fall or like Christ after the resurrection?

2. How does God's redemptive plan help you to understand the heart of God better?

3. What can you do that not even the angel Gabriel can do?

Meditation 3

The Ark as a Type of Christ

Then the Lord said to Noah, 'Go into the ark, you and all your household, for I have seen that you are righteous before me in this generation. Take with you seven pairs of all clean animals, the male and his mate, and a pair of the animals that are not clean, the male and his mate, and seven pairs of the birds of the heavens also, male and female, to keep their offspring alive on the face of all the earth. For in seven days I will send rain on the earth forty days and forty nights, and every living thing that I have made I will blot out from the face of the ground.' And Noah did all that the Lord had commanded him.

—Genesis 7:1.

It just so happened that I was in the visitor centre at Bannockburn not long after the release of the movie *Braveheart*. For those not familiar with either the movie or the battlefield, Bannockburn, located just outside Stirling in Scotland, was the scene of Robert the Bruce's defeat of Edward II's English army. I took the opportunity of asking the knowledgeable tour guide what he thought of Mel Gibson's version of Scottish history. His answer was as simple as it was direct: 'There was a man called William Wallace. The rest is Hollywood.'

I was put in mind of his response many years later when I saw the movie that purports to be about Noah. 'Ah,' I thought to myself, 'there was a man called Noah. The rest is Hollywood.' Indeed, so far removed from the biblical narrative was the movie that I was surprised Hollywood had managed to spell his name correctly! Be warned! Don't get your history from watching a movie. And, more importantly, don't get your theology from that source either!

By contrast the biblical narrative of Noah and the flood is a much-loved story that rightly has been the staple of Sunday School teachers for generations. The picture of the animals going into the ark two by two has always captured the imagination of children young and old. And not only children! The story is simple and beautiful.

We are still only a few chapters into the storyline of the Bible, but following the fall there is no evidence of widespread deep remorse coupled with a desire to show contrition. There was no attempt to repair the damage sin had done. The testimony of God is clear: He 'saw that the wickedness of man was great in the earth, and that every intention of the thoughts of his heart was only evil continually' (Gen. 6:5). With that as the context, the opening verses of chapter 6 draw our attention to the continuing rebellion against God. The 'sons of God saw that the daughters of man were attractive. And they took as their wives any they chose.'

The meaning and interpretation of that verse and surrounding ones are many and in some cases nothing short of astonishing. The curiosity the verse and its interpretations provokes may distract us from the echo of a previous verse in which Eve *saw* that the fruit was *good* and *took* it in the first act of rebellion. 'Saw,' 'good,' and 'take' are all found in both verses. The rebellion, that every intention of the thoughts of man's heart was only evil continually, warns us that here is a world ripe for judgment. When God comes to pronounce his sentence on a world in rebellion, his sentence is just.

However, even in the earliest chapters of Genesis, God displays an attribute which is taken note of by the Psalmist, who also delights in it: God is 'slow to anger.' If God were to send a wind to keep apart the waters of the Red Sea to allow the Children of Israel under the leadership of Moses to pass through safely, we can confidently assume that any number of other measures were open to God to preserve the lives of Noah and his family (not to mention the guarantee of his promise that the seed of the woman would bruise the head of the serpent). But God did not use an immediate and dramatic intervention to protect Noah. We should not allow our familiarity with the story to rob us of the curious means that God appoints. He tells Noah to build an ark. And not just any ark, but an ark so large that it was not surpassed in size until the Industrial Revolution of the nineteenth century.

How long did it take Noah and his sons to build the ark? There are a number of estimates. Perhaps as much as one hundred and twenty years! But there's another curious fact about Noah. When the apostle Peter speaks of him in his epistle, he describes him not as a shipwright but as a 'preacher of righteousness.' The two are by no means mutually exclusive—no more than describing Paul as a 'tentmaker' and also 'the Apostles to the Gentiles.' It does, however, help us understand how he went about his God-given task.

I don't believe it is imposing anything on the text to suppose that as he went to the local lumber yard to pick up yet another consignment of wood, that he would be asked what he needed it for. The more he bought and the longer he and his sons built, the greater the curiosity aroused. Perhaps the first few times when he explained that he was building an ark, he would have been stared at in disbelief, or received an irritated, 'All right then, don't tell me, if you don't want to. It's your business!' But as the ark took shape it would have become evident that Noah was indeed building a massive ship. 'So why are you building a ship so far from the sea, Noah?' And Noah, always ready to give a reason for the hope that was in him, would explain that God, who is righteous, was going to bring destruction on a world in rebellion. Day by day, week by week, month by month, year by year, in word and in deed, Noah bore testimony to the righteousness of God. But the very length of time it took Noah to complete his task bore testimony to God's desire for men to repent and not to be damned.

Though none but Noah and the seven members of his family knew it, they were living in a day of grace. Judgment was coming, but God had raised up a preacher of righteousness to warn a wicked generation. Many centuries later in the great city of Nineveh, such a message led to the repentance of the king and his subjects. In one sense we could say that the story need not to have ended as it did. But there was no such melting of the heart among Noah's contemporaries.

No doubt the doings of 'Nutty Noah' were noised abroad. You can almost imagine the conversation in neighbouring valleys:

'What shall we do this afternoon, Dad?'

'Let's go and see what Nutty Noah is doing! I hear he is building a boat.'

'A boat! But we are miles away from any water. Why's he doing that?'

'He thinks God is going to bring a great flood and he's getting ready!'

'Dad, do you think he's safe? I mean, crazy people can be dangerous!'

When Nehemiah rebuilt the walls of Jerusalem, the unbelievers laughed at him, saying, that if even a fox climbed on it the wall would fall down. The first weapon drawn against preachers is often ridicule. Laughed at or not, Noah continued faithfully to build.

At last the ark was built and God brought its cargo to Noah. The laughter must have changed to perplexed curiosity as all sorts of animals, and I mean *all sorts* of animals, made their way to the ark. 'Well, how did he manage that?' 'Where are all those animals coming from?' 'What is making them come to Noah's ark?'

Recounting the story there are so many applications that spring to mind. One can see in Noah a man who continued faithful, and in the estimation of Scripture is more remembered for his preaching than for his ship-building abilities. One can also see from the story that the message was of what the old Puritans would have called 'the exceeding sinfulness of sin.' In spite of faithful preaching that warned of the judgment to come, none heeded the message.

Contrariwise, we see God preserving Noah and his family, and with him the multitude of species, each after its kind. It's a wonderful story and quite rightly delights the ears of children.

But do we only turn to the Old Testament as a source of stories which illustrate this virtue or that, providing a vivid picture of a particular vice, coupled with a warning? 'Now children, the people in Noah's day didn't listen to the preacher and look what happened to them!' Tempting though such a conclusion is (especially to preachers), it is perhaps not the most helpful application, and it is certainly not the most important.

God did indeed preserve the life of Noah, his wife, his sons and their wives, and a multitude of animals. But *God is always better than we can imagine.*

Contained in the story is not only God's justice but his grace. Not only was righteousness preached by Noah day after day, and year after year, but righteousness was preached by the very ark itself. The story is so much more than an illustration of certain sad aspects of a fallen world. The ark itself is the message. Yes, Noah's preaching focused on the justice of God—judgement was going to fall on man because of the continuously evil intentions of the thoughts of his heart; but Noah also declared in his preaching that God was preparing a way of escape. In Noah's day the alternatives could not have been more dramatic or more obvious. When the waters of judgment came the ark was the only place of safety. To be outside of the ark was to fall under the judgment of God.

Is that so different to the message of the gospel we proclaim? Though preachers are ridiculed to this day, those who are faithful still proclaim that the only place of refuge from the coming judgement of God is 'in Christ.' To be outside of Christ is to be lost. To die outside of Christ is to die without hope.

But there is more. *God is always better than we can imagine.*

On the very day the first drops of rain fell, Noah entered the ark with his wife, sons and daughters-in-law, and the Lord shut them in. It was the same rain that fell upon the ark as fell upon that wicked generation. When the water of God's judgment fell, it fell on Noah to his salvation, but to the destruction of those who were outside of the ark. And how is the work of redemption applied to those who are Christ's? Paul never hesitates to speak of believers being 'in Christ.' When our beloved

Redeemer went to the cross the wrath of a righteous God was revealed from heaven against all unrighteousness. But when God's justice was measured out in all its awesome severity, those 'in Christ' were lifted up to salvation, but those who remain outside of Christ must needs perish.

But this is yet the day of grace. Preachers still proclaim the righteousness of God. They are still preaching God's grace. It is a solemn truth that God will bring his judgment to bear upon a world which continues in rebellion against him, but he still sends preachers to plead with sinners to come to Christ who is, in the words of Thomas Brooks, the Puritan preacher, 'an ark for all God's Noahs.'

You, dear reader! If a friend has placed this book in your hand and you have read thus far out of curiosity or for some other reason, I would urge you to consider whether you are *in Christ*. The door of the ark is wide open. The judgment of God will not long be delayed; but here is the gracious invitation. All those who come to Jesus he will never cast out (cf. John 6:37). In a wicked generation the gospel was preached, and it is still being preached because our God is a God of grace' (cf. Psa. 103:8).

For further reflection:

1. What was *Noah* doing while he was building the ark?

2. What was *God* doing while Noah was building the ark?

3. Why do you think God delayed so long in bringing judgment upon the world?

Meditation 4

My Word Is My Bond

Behold, my covenant is with you, and you shall be the father of a multitude of nations. No longer shall your name be called Abram, but your name shall be Abraham, for I have made you the father of a multitude of nations. I will make you exceedingly fruitful, and I will make you into nations, and kings shall come from you. And I will establish my covenant between me and you and your offspring after you throughout their generations for an everlasting covenant, to be God to you and to your offspring after you. And I will give to you and to your offspring after you the land of your sojournings, all the land of Canaan, for an everlasting possession, and I will be their God.

—Genesis 17:4-8.

When I was a small boy I was taken on a visit to the London Stock Exchange. And when I say *small*, I think I was only nine at the time. My dear old mum never missed an opportunity to improve my education, usually it seemed, acting under the conviction that if you throw enough mud at a wall some of it will stick. Something did stick from that visit to the Stock Exchange but to be honest, only one thing. I remember being impressed by the fact that the brokers on the Stock Exchange floor made their bargains with one another without the exchange of documents or any other written pledges. Their motto, I was told, was simply 'My word is my bond.' It is strange to think that a simple five-word statement can be written on the memory from a single telling, while many a hapless teacher has made shipwreck of his talents by repeatedly trying to force into my memory other and sometimes shorter maxims.

God, of course, has no need to write down his pledge to Abram, but he does employ a rather singular means to keep his word ever before the great 'father of the faithful:' God changes Abram's name! No more would he be called 'Abram;' from that day on his name would be 'Abraham' because the Lord had made him a father of nations. Every time anyone addressed him, the promise would be restated. Perhaps common use day after day would lessen the impact of the name change even on Abraham himself, but the promise of God was always before him nonetheless.

But it is not the change of name that I find most arresting. It is the fact that God declares that he has made his servant a father of many nations. As all Bible students know, Abraham would have to wait many years before Isaac would be born. The fulfilment would be some time in coming. In fact, Abraham would not see the things promised by God in his lifetime. His son, Isaac would not see much of the promise's fulfilment either. He had only Esau and Jacob and they seemed more intent on killing each other than becoming great nations. When, at last, Joseph closed Jacob's eyes in death, there was a glimmer of hope's realisation in the greater fulfilment that would come during the four centuries of exile in the land of Egypt as the Children of Israel did indeed grow to be a great nation.

When a Pharaoh arose who did not know Joseph it may have seemed to many an Israelite as though God had forgotten them. The book of Exodus is a long and detailed statement that he had not. Dramatic and compelling though the story of the exodus from Egypt is, it would make no sense without the final chapters of Genesis telling us just how the Children of Israel came to be in Egypt in the first place.

A severe famine had wracked Egypt and indeed the countries far beyond its borders. Jacob had been compelled to send his sons into Egypt to buy food for themselves and for their livestock. The story is well enough known of how Joseph's brothers sold him as a slave but how God raised him up to be prime minister of Egypt. It is striking that as Joseph goes from being favoured son to slave to prisoner, that the word of God emphasizes (four times in Gen. 39) that *the Lord was with him*. Joseph didn't waver from that conviction either. How do we know? He held with confidence to God's revealed word given to him in a dream that one day his brothers would bow before him. Now that may seem a bit of a stretch: how can we possibly know that? When the Pharoah's chief cupbearer and baker had their dreams, Joseph's response was to tell them that God is the one who interprets dreams, and Joseph asks the servants of Pharaoh to tell him theirs! He didn't say, 'I had a couple of dreams a long time ago and was really sure I understood them, but, alas, they came to nothing.' No, his response to the cupbearer and baker was, 'Tell me your dreams!' The faith of Abraham burned brightly in his great-grandson.

Later on, when his brothers were alarmed at the turn of events as Joseph revealed himself to them, he sought to reassure them by pointing them to the sovereignty of God. Whatever the intentions, 'God meant it for good' (Gen. 50:20). Joseph had been sent to Egypt to preserve life. Bringing the Children of Israel out of Egypt with a mighty hand and outstretched arm was not the only demonstration of God's sovereignty and grace. The reader cannot do justice to the Scriptures without seeing that God was no less behind taking Jacob and his children into Egypt than he was in their departure.

But there is more in the story. We are accustomed to thinking of the concluding chapters of Genesis as the story of Joseph. I think a close reading of the text will show that God is not just with Joseph but with his brothers too. If God has been sustaining Joseph through his trials, he has also been working on the brothers to bring them to the point where Judah, speaking for them all, declares that he will bear the penalty if any evil comes upon Benjamin. Miracles of grace have taken place in hard hearts so that those who were once so filled with bitterness at the preferential treatment shown to one of their brothers, are now willing to yield themselves for their youngest brother who seems no less to have been accorded a privileged position by their father Jacob.

For those with eyes to see, God was showing himself gracious to the godly Joseph and the less than godly Judah and his brethren. But there was surely more. God had promised to make Abraham into a great nation: a promise so sure as to be stated in the perfect tense—a completed action—even though Abraham did not see the promise fulfilled. Neither did his son Isaac see it fulfilled. Nor did his grandson Jacob see it fulfilled in his lifetime. But during those long centuries in exile from the Promised Land, imperceptibly at first, Jacob's family grew into a great nation—so great in fact that Pharaoh feared for his throne and the stability of his kingdom. Generations had come and gone but the purposes of God were ripening fast.

In the midst of oppression and heavy trials the Children of Israel may not have had as firm a grasp on the promises of God as they should. We don't say this to accuse them but to recognize that *their* frailty is *our* frailty too. I have to confess *I* need frequent reminders that God not only has made promises but that he is fulfilling them, and that the evidence of that is before my eyes if I would but open them.

God made a promise to his servant Abraham that he had made of him many nations. While our circumstances might often remind us that we are living in a fallen world, the gospel is being preached and people on every continent of the earth are being gathered out of all nations to worship him. It was while they were in exile that God was at work to multiply the Children of Israel into a great nation.

One wonders how Abraham thought of the promise of God; how did he envisage its fulfilment? But there is more to the promise of God, for *God is always better than we can imagine*. God promises Abraham that kings would come from him.

If Scripture is to be taken seriously then the splendour of the court of King Solomon was beyond imagination. Even a contemporary ruler, the Queen of Sheba, had her breath taken away at what she saw when brought into Solomon's majestic presence and given an audience with the king. One wonders if Abraham the nomad who dwelt in tents could have imagined the royal grandeur which his descendant Solomon enjoyed. Indeed, no matter how often he thought about the scope of the promise, he would have found it impossible to see fully the 'many nations' to 'the ends of the earth' that now consider him 'the father of the faithful.'

Be that as it may, how magnificently, how gloriously does God fulfil his promise! But there is more for *God is always better than we can imagine*. From Abraham came a king greater than Solomon—the Lord Jesus

Christ—whose kingdom knows no end. I wonder, did Abraham understand that God in Christ would become flesh and that he, the greatest of all of the descendants of Abraham, would sit on a throne and rule over the world for ever, having been given a name that is above every name, and at whose name every knee shall bow and every tongue confess that he is Lord?

If the Queen of Sheba was so overwhelmed by the splendour of Solomon that her breath was taken away, how shall we respond when we see the King of kings in all his glory? He is, after all, better than we can imagine.

For further reflection:

1. How much of God's promise to Abraham was fulfilled during his lifetime?

2. Where did God begin to fulfil his promise to make of Abraham a great nation?

3. How much greater will the final fulfilment of God's promises be compared to what we can see presently?

Meditation 5

Oh that Ishmael Might Live before You!

And God said to Abraham, 'As for Sarai your wife, you shall not call her name Sarai, but Sarah shall be her name. I will bless her, and moreover, I will give you a son by her. I will bless her, and she shall become nations; kings of peoples shall come from her.' Then Abraham fell on his face and laughed and said to himself, 'Shall a child be born to a man who is a hundred years old? Shall Sarah, who is ninety years old, bear a child?' And Abraham said to God, 'Oh that Ishmael might live before you!' God said, 'No, but Sarah your wife shall bear you a son, and you shall call his name Isaac. I will establish my covenant with him as an everlasting covenant for his off-spring after him. As for Ishmael, I have heard you; behold, I have blessed him and will make him fruitful and multiply him greatly. He shall father twelve princes, and I will make him into a great nation. But I will establish my covenant with Isaac, whom Sarah shall bear to you at this time next year. —Genesis 17:15-21.

I remember hearing of someone who undertook a speed reading course. At the end of it, he read through Tolstoy's massive work *War and Peace* in fourteen minutes. When asked what it was about, he responded, 'I think it was about Russia.' Well, perhaps for those of lesser ability (among whom I count myself), the slow approach is the better to allow time for the material to sink in. But at least the speed reader did grasp the one central aspect of that great story. As a general rule, the more space a book devotes to a particular subject or character the more significant it is for the development of the story.

If we go to the beginning of the Bible we only have eleven chapters (nine pages in the Bible I have in front of me) to get from God alone (quite literally), through creation, the fall, the first murder, the flood, and the tower of Babel. The end of chapter 11 introduces us to Abraham (still at that time known as 'Abram'), and we remain in his company until his death in Genesis 25. At that point the Bible has spent more column inches on Abraham than on the rest of the history of mankind put together.

With such a long and significant life there are many ways in which we might develop our theme ('God is always better than we can imagine'). However, I would like us to reflect on Abraham and Ishmael. In the next meditation we will consider Abraham and Isaac.

Chapter 17 opens with the Lord appearing to Abraham and renewing his covenant with him. At this point in the story Abraham is ninety-nine years old. It has been some twenty-four years since God told him to leave Haran for the land of promise. Those intervening years must not have been easy for Abraham. He knew the ultimate goal—his destiny—but the way ahead was not clear to him. Though God had promised him a lasting posterity, there really wasn't much of a tangible indication of its realization. Sarah was well past the age of bearing children. Therefore she tried to help God out by giving her handmaid Hagar to Abraham. Hagar bore Abraham a son, Ishmael. Now Abraham had a son. Was it not reasonable for Abraham and Sarah to expect that God's promises would be fulfilled in and through him?

Perhaps it is not so surprising, after all that had happened, that the Lord should appear again to Abraham, to encourage him. Even the Lord's opening greeting to Abraham is instructive. The Lord appeared to Abraham announcing himself to be 'God Almighty.' Though there was not much evidence of it at the time, God renewed his promise that he would greatly increase Abraham's numbers.

In what follows, God lays out in some detail what he will do. Even a casual reading of these verses makes clear that it is God who will be taking the lead. The number of first person plural pronouns ('I') in the text whiz past like telegraph poles on the road of blessing. Here's a slightly edited text to give us the gist:

> This is my covenant with you.
> You will be the father of many nations.
> No longer will you be called Abram but Abraham.

I have made you a father of many nations.
I will make you very fruitful.
I will make nations of you and kings will come from you.
I will establish my covenant as an everlasting covenant between me and your descendants.
I will give an everlasting possession to you and to your descendants.
I will be their God.

Whether or not Abraham needed to hear the renewal of God's gracious promises, God reaffirmed them nonetheless. But God goes further: he tells Abraham explicitly what he had not told him before, that Sarah would be the one through whom the promises would be fulfilled. So the promises of God continue.

I will bless her and surely give you a son by her.
I will bless her so that she shall be the mother of nations; kings of peoples shall come from her.

Sarah was not to be merely a spectator of the blessings of her husband but would be intimately involved in their delivery. Later on Sarah will laugh at the promise, but not before Abraham does the same! He fell on his face and in his heart questioned God: 'Will a son be born to a man a hundred years old? Will Sarah bear a child at the age of ninety?'

Abraham was not doubting that God would fulfil his promise, but the means seemed—well—unrealistic. He asked God instead, 'Oh that Ishmael might live before you!' Perhaps less strictly accurate but with a better sense of the original, this request might be translated, 'If only Ishmael might live under your blessing!'

We may be strong in faith to believe that God will in the end accomplish all that he purposes, but weak in faith to trust with regard to the means God will use. For example, why is there an emphasis in some evangelical circles on drama in place of the sermon? Might it not come from the fact that evangelical believers have lost confidence in the power of the pulpit? The preaching of the word of God has not been anointed with the out-pouring of the Spirit as in previous generations, so like Sarah we give God a helping hand: 'What we need are better techniques. Let's use the latest video technology for presenting the gospel. Let's give people something to look at!' But faith comes *by hearing*, or so the Bible says (Rom. 10:17). It is the 'foolishness of preaching' that God uses to convert sinful people (1 Cor. 1:21). Perhaps preaching is simply meant to be foolish, so that all might know that the conversion of a sinner was accomplished by the power of Spirit of the living God, and not because the preacher used all the latest presentational techniques to manipulate his audience.

At this point in the story of Abraham, though he believed God's promises, there was a doubt in his heart regarding the means that God said he would use. But *God is always better than we can imagine.*

Spurgeon gave a memorable illustration of this very thing—our need to trust God's wisdom in the *means* as well as the *end*. He told a story about a little German boy. This little fellow believed God and delighted in prayer. His teacher had often stressed the importance of being punctual in his attendance at school and the young lad tried to be so. His parents, however, were not so careful about time-keeping, and on one occasion, through no fault of his own, the little boy found himself leaving the house just as the hour was struck when he should be at school. The boy prayed, 'Dear God, grant that I may be in time for school.' Now anyone hearing that prayer might have concluded that this was a prayer that would have to go unanswered. For the boy had some distance to walk to the school and the hour had already struck. His situation was not so different to that of Abraham. How could God possibly fulfil the means given that Sarah was already 90?

Spurgeon continued the story. It so happened that that morning the teacher had turned the key in the lock the wrong way and could not move the bolt. The teacher had had to send for a locksmith who opened the door just as the young fellow arrived; and so he was able to enter the school with the rest of his fellow pupils.

As God said to Sarah when declaring his promise in her hearing, 'Is anything too hard for the LORD?'

For further reflection:

1. Do you find yourself tempted at times to 'help God out' in the fulfilment of his promises?

2. In what ways do you sometimes think you can improve on what God says?

3. Where should your confidence lie?

Meditation 6

God Will Provide for Himself the Lamb

After these things God tested Abraham and said to him, 'Abraham!' And he said, 'Here am I.' He said, 'Take your son, your only son Isaac, whom you love, and go to the land of Moriah, and offer him there as a burnt offering on one of the mountains of which I shall tell you.' So Abraham rose early in the morning, saddled his donkey, and took two of his young men with him, and his son Isaac. And he cut the wood for the burnt offering and arose and went to the place of which God had told him. On the third day Abraham lifted up his eyes and saw the place from afar. Then Abraham said to his young men, 'Stay here with the donkey; I and the boy will go over there and worship and come again to you.' And Abraham took the wood of the burnt offering and laid it on Isaac his son. And he took in his hand the fire and the knife. So they went both of them together. And Isaac said to his father Abraham, 'My father!' And he said, 'Here am I, my son.' He said, 'Behold, the fire and the wood, but where is the lamb for a burnt offering?' Abraham said, 'God will provide for himself the lamb for a burnt offering, my son.' So they went both of them together. —Genesis 22:1-8.

God will always keep his promises. He will not always keep them in the way or according to the time scale that we expect. Take God's promises to Abraham. He had called Abraham out of Ur of the Chaldees. Actually, it was Abraham's father Terah who led the family out of Ur to go to Canaan; but they only got as far as Haran which is where Terah died. It was at this point that the Lord appeared to Abraham and told him to leave Haran for the land that he was going to show him. Moreover, he also promised to make of Abraham a great nation. Abraham believed God and it was counted to him as righteousness. As we read the story thousands of years later, it is clear that God kept his promise to Abraham. Not only did God make a nation out of Abraham's descendants, but it was from that nation that God raised up the promised Messiah Jesus Christ.

What may not be clear without a close reading of the central section of the book of Genesis is just how much Abraham trusted the Lord, and how little he actually saw of the fulfilment of the promises in his own lifetime. The Scriptures happily fix certain key events by telling us how old Abraham was at a particular time. When God promised to make of him a great nation, he was seventy-five years old. Not to put too fine a point on it, it would appear that God was in no hurry to fulfil the promise. A decade slipped by, and Abraham expressed his concern to the Lord that he had as yet no child, and that his servant Eliezar of Damascus was likely to inherit all that belonged to Abraham after his death.

God assured Abraham that Eliezar would not be his heir. His own son would inherit everything. It is at this point that God took Abraham outside and showed him the night sky. If Abraham could count the number of all the stars then he would be able to count the number of all his descendants. A magnificent promise for sure, but Sarah was still without child.

So what are we to do when God is not working according to our timetable? Are we not tempted to do what Sarah did: we give God a helping hand. She gave Abraham her handmaid Hagar as a wife, with the result that at the age of eighty-six Abraham became a father at long last. The son born to Hagar he named Ishmael.

Perhaps, with a baby in the household, the promise was now secure and Abraham could settle down with his two wives to enjoy whatever time he had left in this world. A knowledge of human nature, if not a working knowledge of the Bible, inform us that Abraham was highly unlikely to find peace in such a household. Hagar, as the mother of Abraham's son and heir, started to assume precedence over her former mistress, much to the fury of Sarah. Perhaps taking shortcuts with God's promises wasn't such a good idea after all!

A further thirteen years were to pass before God

renewed his promise to make a great nation out of Abraham. God's promise was now more explicit than before: it was to be through a son born to Sarah that the fulfilment of God's gracious purposes would be made known; not through Hagar's son Ishmael. The problem that both Abraham and Sarah could see all too clearly was that by this time Abraham was ninety-nine and Sarah ninety years of age. Sarah had abandoned the hope of having a child decades earlier. Indeed, it had been close to a quarter of a century since God had made the promise to make of Abraham a great nation and so far all he had to show for it was the thirteen-year-old Ishmael. Counting the stars in the night sky presented a great challenge to Abraham, but counting his offspring was not so difficult!

But when God makes a promise, he keeps it. For his hundredth birthday Sarah presented her husband with a son, Isaac. At last, approximately twenty-five years after God had originally made the promise, Abraham had a son by Sarah.

But why, at every point in the story, is there such an emphasis on Abraham's age? The obvious conclusion is that Abraham was not so much *getting old*, but *had become old*. He had entered on the great adventure of faith at an age when most of us enter retirement. But there is something else. Abraham was getting older and older still. The seventy-five-year-old quickly becomes the one hundred-year-old before the first unmistakable evidence of the fulfilment of God's promise is seen sitting on his knee.

More years pass and Isaac has become a young lad. It is at this point in the story that the inexplicable and the irresistible breaks in. God tells Abraham to take his son, his only son, the son whom he loves, and offer him to God as a burnt offering. There is no mention of Abraham's age in this part of the story. Nor need there be. That point has already been well made. The focus of God's promise is unmistakable. God had promised Abraham that Isaac would be the one through whom his promises would be fulfilled. But the command of God was as clear as the promise in Isaac was undeniable: Abraham must offer 'the son of the promise' to God as a burnt offering.

A burnt offering, as the opening chapter of Leviticus makes clear, is one that is offered to make atonement. But perhaps, at this point, to ask what it was that Abraham was atoning for is to rush unfeelingly by the deep distress of soul through which Abraham must have passed.

Hebrews 11 — that great chapter on the heroes of the faith — simply reports that Abraham was willing to offer up Isaac because he believed that the Lord was able to raise him from the dead: that is what God did, figuratively speaking.

We shouldn't let the simplicity of the words blind us to the momentous nature of the command God gave Abraham. The promise God made to Abraham had taken decades to fulfil. Isaac had grown into a young lad. It was when the fulfilment of God's promise seemed most secure that the word came to 'take your son, your only son, the son whom you love …' O how every clause falls like a hammer on the anvil of the father's tender heart. The Septuagint (the early Greek translation of the Hebrew Scriptures) goes even further: 'take your son, your only son, *your beloved son* which you love ...'

We are told that Abraham rose early the next morning, saddled the donkey, organized two servants and his son, and split some wood for the offering, which apparently he did himself. There was no delay. The command was clear and Abraham's obedience was promptly given.

The destination was no secret. The command was to go to Mount Moriah. Later Mount Moriah would be known as Mount Zion, in the City of David, Jerusalem. Centuries later another will set his face towards that very place, full of the knowledge of what lay before him (Luke 9:51, 53).

It seems unlikely that there would have been much conversation on the three days it took them to reach their destination. Abraham left his servants a little distance away and took only Isaac with him the final part of the journey. It is Isaac who breaks the silence. He was carrying the wood and his father was carrying the fire, but where was the lamb going to come from for the burnt offering?

Abraham prophetically told his son that God would provide, or select, for himself the lamb for the burnt offering.

They walked on together.

At last they came to the appointed place and made an altar, laying the wood on the rough stones before Abraham laid the boy who had dutifully carried the wood up

Mount Moriah. Faithfully obedient to the last, Abraham raised the knife to 'slaughter his son' when a voice from heaven stayed his hand.

A ram, providentially held fast in a thicket by its horns, was at hand and became the substitutionary sacrifice. So the life of Abraham's son, his only son, the beloved son whom he loved, was spared that day.

The writer of the letter to the Hebrews (as well as the Genesis narrative) does not hesitate to state—whether we find it a comfortable idea or not—that God was testing Abraham in this episode. There are times when our faith is likewise put to the test. Is that ever a pleasant experience? Surely not! But that shouldn't really come as a surprise to us for in the Bible the testing of our faith is likened to a 'refining fire.' Precious metals such as gold or silver must be heated to very high temperatures if they are to have their impurities removed. So God will at times place us in a fiery furnace to purify us for his glory and for our eternal good. Shadrach, Meshach and Abednego famously went through a fiery furnace when Nebuchadnezzar persecuted them, but they were not harmed by the experience, for we are told: 'The hair of their heads was not singed, their cloaks were not harmed, and no smell of fire had come upon them' (Dan. 3:27).[1] God's refining fire will do us no harm: 'In this [salvation] you rejoice, though now for a little while, if necessary,

---

[1] For more on Shadrach, Meshach and Abednego see Meditation 16.

you have been grieved by various trials, so that the tested genuineness of your faith—more precious than gold that perishes though it is tested by fire—may be found to result in praise and glory and honour at the revelation of Jesus Christ' (1 Pet. 1:6, 7).

However, if all we can see in Genesis 22 is the implacable commitment of Abraham then we have missed some of the greatest comforts this passage has to offer. For *God is always better than we can imagine.*

Perhaps you may have already noted some connections which point us to Jesus, the one in whom all nations shall be blessed.

God called for a sacrifice of atonement—the burnt offering. The place of fulfilment by God's appointing was Mount Moriah, also known as Mount Zion. The son, the only son, the son whom the Father loved, carried the wood on which he was to be sacrificed. One cannot help but see the parallels. But with one notable exception: the hand of Abraham was stayed and Isaac's life was spared. God, on the other hand did not spare his one and only Son, but freely offered him up for us all. Abraham rightly stands before us as the father of the faithful, who by his own example encourages us to be ever faithful. Without taking anything away from his actions, we surely see that his faithfulness does but reflect the God who defines faithfulness. The hand of the Father was not stayed when it laid the awesome weight of divine justice upon his one and only Son.

But there is more.

Paul draws a wonderfully comforting conclusion from the Father's willingness to lay the heavy load on his own Son. If God did not spare his own Son, but gave him up for us all, how will he not along with him freely give us all things?

When we receive Christ, we receive all things.

For further reflection:

1. Does God answer your prayers in your time or in his?

2. What does the story of Abraham and Isaac teach us about God?

3. If God did not spare his own son, but freely gave him up for us all, what will God also give us along with him?

Meditation 7

Jacob Prays for Bread but Returns with Flocks and Herds

So early in the morning Jacob took the stone that he had put under his head and set it up for a pillar and poured oil on the top of it. He called the name of that place Bethel, but the name of the city was Luz at the first. Then Jacob made a vow, saying, 'If God will be with me and will keep me in this way that I go, and will give me bread to eat and clothing to wear, so that I come again to my father's house in peace, then the Lord shall be my God, and this stone, which I have set up for a pillar, shall be God's house. And of all that you give me I will give a full tenth to you.' — Genesis 28:18-22.

In our previous meditation, as we were thinking about Abraham and Sarah, we noted that Sarah in particular seemed to have succumbed to the temptation of helping God out with his plans. That sounds a bit foolish, doesn't it, as though God can use a little assistance from us from time to time? In one way, however, there is a positive. It does mean that we are actually expecting God ultimately to keep his promises. It is just the means that are not quite so fixed in our minds. It may be that Sarah had passed on that defective way of thinking to her daughter-in-law Rebecca, or, perhaps more likely, Rebecca had the same weakness most of us share in too.

So let us think a little about Rebecca, before we turn our attention to her husband Jacob. Like her mother-in-law before her, Rebecca had difficulty in conceiving. Though it may not provide much comfort, the theme is touched on frequently in Scripture, but we will return to this subject in Meditation 12.

Rebecca, as well as Sarah, were both considered to be barren. Were they not therefore a strange choice then for God? There are repeated promises of descendants as numerous as grains of sand on the seashore, but Sarah has only one son whom she bears at ninety. Isaac married his second cousin Rebecca when he was forty, but did not start a family straight away, for we read of Isaac praying for his 'barren' wife that she might have children (Gen. 25:21). That means that Abraham was 140 years old when his son got married. Perhaps we can sympathize with Abraham because the fulfilment of God's promises was far from instantaneous. Many years passed while he waited patiently to see them fulfilled.

Isaac prayed to the Lord and, by his grace, Rebecca conceived twins. While still in their mother's womb the babies jostled with each other, causing Rebecca to inquire of the Lord why this was happening to her. The response was a promise of great blessing to her: 'Two nations are in your womb, and two peoples from within you shall be divided; the one shall be stronger than the other, the older shall serve the younger' (Gen. 25:23).

Was it because God seemed to favour the younger or was it because he grew up more at home 'among the tents,' a quieter lad than his outdoor-loving brother, that Rebecca favoured Jacob over Esau? The family dynamic must have been as interesting as it was unhealthy. The father favoured the firstborn, rough and ready Esau; the mother favoured the younger son, smooth and sly Jacob. When did Jacob first learn about the terms of God's promise, that his tough hunter brother would serve him? Perhaps when he was still quite young. I don't know if it did much to improve their relationship. Most likely it led to Jacob despising his older brother—after all, one day he would be his superior and every one would know it.

Events even seemed to work in Jacob's favor. His brother came in from the fields one day and he was starving. Jacob, always close to home, was preparing some food which Esau was eager to have. Familial affection should have led Jacob to share the food with his sibling, but instead he saw a golden opportunity for gain and an occasion to help God along in the fulfilment of his promise. In exchange for a bowl of stew Esau sold his birthright to the wily Jacob. It is a sad tale of dysfunctional family life and it shows neither of the young men in a good light. Jacob is manipulative, and always has an eye to the main chance. Esau, who thought so lightly of the blessing belonging to the oldest son, and governed by his appetite, sells what is precious for a bowl of stew and a moment's gratification. The Scriptures are truthful, sometimes painfully so.

Many years pass and Isaac, now an old man, thinks his time is almost over. He asks Esau to go out hunting for his favourite meat and then prepare a tasty meal for his father. Following the meal he will give Esau the blessing of the firstborn. However, Rebecca overhears the conversation. She decides to turn it to the advantage of her favourite son Jacob. And, of course, why not? Hasn't God promised that 'the older will serve the younger'? If Jacob can make sure of the blessing that really belongs to the older son, then all was sure to work out perfectly in the end. After all, God had already told Rebecca what he intended to do. So all she was doing was just helping him out a little.

Reading through the account we just know that the story is not taking a turn for the better. Esau not noted for his gentle godly ways, promises himself that as soon as his father dies, he shall get his own back on that scheming little brother of his. Somewhat in keeping with his tough exterior, Esau saw no need to keep his plan a secret, and word reached Rebecca's ears, who then informs her favourite son. There was nothing else for it. Jacob must leave town or Rebecca would be burying a son as well as a husband.

Jacob flees from his angry brother, but in which direction? He sets out for Haran, the very town from which

God had called his grandfather, Abraham, a couple of centuries earlier. Abraham had had Ishmael and then Isaac. Ishmael had had twelve sons, but they couldn't get along with Isaac's side of the family. Isaac had had two sons, Esau and Jacob, and they couldn't get along with each other either, and the one through whom the promise was to be fulfilled was heading back to the very place where Abraham had started out. This is not a success story in which every event adds to the glory of what has gone before.

Has God forgotten his promises?

What are we to think of Jacob? He does not appear to be the most pleasant of characters. *Scheming* and *deceitful* seem more appropriate descriptions of him than *godly* and *good*. After tricking Isaac into giving him the blessing which his father had intended to give Esau, he has to flee for his life. Though we do not condone the murderous intent of Esau, we can somewhat understand his anger. We hope that if we were in his shoes we would not have decided to kill Jacob; but it has to be said that Jacob has been largely responsible of the alienation of his brother.

So we follow the story to the episode where we see Jacob, the boy who liked to stay around the tents, now sleeping out under the starry sky. It is there, while on the run for his life, that God gave him a dream of angels ascending and descending from earth to heaven. God went further, and told Jacob that he was the God of Abraham and of Isaac, and that he promised to give to Jacob and his descendants the land on which he was lying. Now, surely this has to be an act of sheer grace. (Esau isn't a particularly attractive character, but he may, in his rather crass and blunt way, be somewhat preferable to Jacob. His father certainly thought so.)

God also renewed the promise he had originally made to Abraham that his descendants would be numerous. But there is a subtlety about the wording as the story of Abraham and his family has progressed. God's first illustration to Abraham is that his descendants should be as numerous *as the stars in heaven*. That gets tempered to as numerous *as the grains of sand on the seashore*. When God speaks to Jacob on this occasion the promise is that his descendants will be *as the dust of the earth*. I don't know about you, but I rather prefer the original promise even if they do amount to much the same thing! The eyes are now directed downward instead of upward into the 'heavens.'

In the light of such a wonderful (not to mention gracious) promise one hopes for something suitable by way of a response. Evidently, there is still much work for grace to do in the life of Jacob. Here's how Jacob replies to God's gracious re-affirmation of the promise made to his grandfather many years earlier: 'If God will be with me and will keep me in this way that I go, and will give me bread to eat and clothing to wear, so that I come again to my father's house in peace, then the LORD shall be my God, and this stone, which I have set up for a pillar, shall be God's house. And of all that you give me I will give a full tenth to you' (Gen. 28:20-22).

It makes you want to smack him! Patriarch or not, what was Jacob thinking of? He was on the run from his own brother who wants to kill him because he has duped his father into giving him his birthright. God graciously re-affirmed the promise made to Abraham and his response is basically to put God on probation: 'That's great, God, but let's just see how you work out first. If you feed me and clothe me and get me back to where I started then, okay, you can be my God.' Because Jacob by character is a schemer he even wanted to try to sweeten the deal by offering a proportion back to God: 'I'll keep 90 per cent for myself, but I'll give you 10 per cent!'

If God were not slow to anger and abounding in steadfast love, that might have been the end of Jacob right there and then. But God *is* slow to anger and full of grace, and *he is always better than we can imagine.*

Jacob asked God to feed and clothe him and bring him back safely. The story does not immediately present his return to us. Jacob had to work fourteen years in the service of his uncle Laban in order to win the hands of his two daughters Leah and Rachel. Laban does not appear to want to help Jacob out just because he is family—no more than Jacob wanted to help Esau out because he was his brother! Jacob is tricked into marrying Leah first of all. Duped, we might say, by a wily relative. Perhaps it just ran in the family. And, perhaps God was putting Jacob on the receiving end of what he had so freely dished out to his father and brother.

If we do not wish to be harsh with Jacob, it may be because at times we recognize ourselves in his story. Sometimes through our scheming we think we can help God fulfil his promises. Sometimes, it may be in the sort of pact that we want to make with him: 'If you do this for me, then I will do this for you.'

So how did God respond to the self-serving and rather offensive offer of a deal? When Jacob eventually returned home his flocks and herds were so great that he thought it best to divide them in two. He went out without a pillow to put under his head and he came back a man of substance with wives and more than a dozen children. It's not just that he didn't deserve any of it; he actually merited God's displeasure.

The story of Jacob compels us to see that God does indeed bless in astonishing ways. More than that: the recipients of God's favour have in no way deserved it. The blessing they enjoy is truly all of grace.

For further reflection:

1. Have you ever found yourself trying to strike a bargain with God?

2. How much of the blessing of God have you earned?

3. What do you owe to God's grace?

Meditation 8

You Meant It for Evil but God Meant It for Good

When Joseph's brothers saw that their father was dead, they said, 'It may be that Joseph will hate us and pay us back for all the evil that we did to him.' So they sent a message to Joseph, saying, 'Your father gave this command before he died, "Say to Joseph, Please forgive the transgression of your brothers and their sin, because they did evil to you." And now, please forgive the transgression of the servants of the God of your father.' Joseph wept when they spoke to him. His brothers also came and fell down before him and said, 'Behold, we are your servants.' But Joseph said to them, 'Do not fear, for am I in the place of God? As for you, you meant evil against me, but God meant it for good, to bring it about that many people should be kept alive, as they are today. So do not fear; I will provide for you and your little ones.' Thus he comforted them and spoke kindly to them.—Genesis 50:15-21.

'You meant evil against me, but God meant it for good.' The words of Joseph to his brothers will be instantly recognizable to not a few of us. How often have we comforted ourselves with this most gracious response? His brothers had understandably grown anxious that on the death of their father Jacob, Joseph would wreak some terrible, even terminal, revenge on them for having plotted his death and then having sold him into slavery. Perhaps, when they were growing up, they had heard the story of how their uncle Esau had nursed his anger against their own father, as he waited for the approaching death of their grandfather Isaac so that he might put an end to the schemer once and for all. Indeed, were there not some disturbing parallels: a son favoured above a sibling by a parent? If the malicious jealousy is not excused, it is, at least, not without a cause.

I say, we have drawn comfort from Joseph's words. Perhaps, by the grace of God (and *only* by the grace of God) we have been brought to confess that our actions or our words have run contrary to our profession. What relief is to be found for our troubled hearts that even our sinful actions, even those of the darkest hue, can be turned by the hand of a sovereign God, not only to *good* but for his greater *glory*, and more! In repentance we yield ourselves to God and humbly recognize that he has not lost control of the situation for a single moment. Though I need hardly say that this acknowledgment provides no warrant for conducting ourselves regardless of an obedient concern for God's revealed will, it does lift our spirits and teaches us to praise the King of kings. Even in our very worst moments, our gracious God remains irrevocably committed to blessing his saints.

Spurgeon had a wonderful illustration of this drawn from the life of Alexander the Great. That mighty conqueror wanted to reward a soldier for his faithful service and told him to go to his treasurer. The soldier demanded such a large sum that the treasurer refused to give it to him, asking him 'How could you be such an unconscionable fellow as to ask so much?' When Alexander heard of it, he agreed with his treasurer that the amount requested was indeed a great sum for the soldier to receive, 'but it is not too much for Alexander to give! He has a high opinion of my greatness. Let him have what he has asked for. I will not fall short of his expectations!' God is a great God, and it is just like him to forgive great sins.

Similarly, these verses in Genesis 50 are like one of those large sacks of grain we might see being delivered to a refugee camp. Once the sack is cut, a torrent of life-sustaining nourishment spills out; and hands rushing to the open tear cannot staunch the flow, but are filled to overflowing. Joseph continues to explain to his brothers the great provision brought so mysteriously about by the divine will: 'to bring it about that many people should be kept alive, as they are today.' Joseph was separated from his brethren, suffered such cruel dislocation, and was exiled from the presence of his father, in order to preserve life. But oh, Christian reader, is that thought not the very joy of your heart—a son separated from his father that many people should be kept alive!

Under the similitude of a dream Joseph foretold that one day his brothers would bend and bow before him. That was realized when they came to Egypt and bowed before Joseph, not recognizing him in his office as the prime minister of Pharaoh. But how much more glorious the day when the tribes of Israel—they who are the spiritual descendants of Abraham—bow before King Jesus and accord him the honour and the praise that is due to him and to him alone! What heart-melting kindness shall we hear from the lips of our great Redeemer on that day? He will declare to us that in spite of our every malicious word or deed, he has meant it for good that many should be kept alive.

But dear friend, stretch forth your hand again to the torn sack, for *God is always better than you can imagine*. As Joseph continued, he gave them such tender assurances of his affection as to allay any lingering concern they might feel. 'So do not fear; I will provide for you and for your little ones!' How might we take those very words to the throne of grace? God has shown his love for us in that while we were still sinners, Christ died for us ungodly sinners (cf. Rom. 5:6-8). Are not the words of Joseph but the echo of the promise of God: 'So do not fear! I will provide for you and for your little ones.'

For further reflection:

1. How great is God's love towards you who believe in Jesus?

2. Do you deserve even the least of God's blessings?

3. Will your lack of merit stop God from blessing you?

Meditation 9

A Mother's Prayer

Now a man from the house of Levi went and took as his wife a Levite woman. The woman conceived and bore a son, and when she saw that he was a fine child, she hid him three months. When she could hide him no longer, she took for him a basket made of bulrushes and daubed it with bitumen and pitch. She put the child in it and placed it among the reeds by the river bank. And his sister stood at a distance to know what would be done to him. Now the daughter of Pharaoh came down to bathe at the river, while her young women walked beside the river. She saw the basket among the reeds and sent her servant woman, and she took it. When she opened it, she saw the child, and behold, the baby was crying. She took pity on him and said, 'This is one of the Hebrews' children.' Then his sister said to Pharaoh's daughter, 'Shall I go and call you a nurse from the Hebrew women to nurse the child for you?' And Pharaoh's daughter said to her, 'Go.' So the girl went and called the child's mother. And Pharaoh's daughter said to her, 'Take this child away and nurse him for me, and I will give you your wages.' So the woman took the child and nursed him. When the child grew up, she brought him to Pharaoh's daughter, and he became her son. She named him Moses, 'Because,' she said, 'I drew him out of the water.'—Exodus 2:1-10.

There can be few griefs to match the sorrow in the heart of a parent who has suffered the loss of a child. Even as I write, I have before me the obituary of a young girl who was 'received into the glory of her Lord Jesus Christ on Sunday evening.' Less than a year before she had been diagnosed with a rare form of cancer. 'By God's enabling grace, over the course of the following ten and a half months, Natalie demonstrated unwavering childlike faith in the goodness of her God. Through her often intense suffering, she was a remarkable example of humble submission to her heavenly Father's tender care and sovereign will. One of Natalie's many prayers was that God would use her life to bring glory to his name. This prayer he has indeed answered. From the most seasoned of Christians to the most simple, all those who prayed, encouraged, supported, wept—and weep—for her, had their hearts drawn upward to give glory to the true and living God, whom to know is life eternal. For this reason, though her family and friends grieve the loss deeply, they also rejoice with joy inexpressible and filled with glory.'

It is hard to read such a testimony and remain unmoved at a life so short, yet so filled with God's grace. It is no less hard to share the sorrow of the parents bereft of a daughter. Without in any sense diminishing the burden imposed on the hearts of the grieving parents, it might serve to open up to us something of the perplexity of spirit in the heart of a mother in ancient Israel.

Jochebed was the wife of Amram and together they already had two children. Their firstborn was Miriam and their second child, was a boy named Aaron. At almost any other time her third pregnancy would have been an occasion of much joy. But this was not any other time. Ominously we are told that a new king had arisen in Egypt who did not know Joseph. The memory of a time when a bright young foreigner had saved the land from catastrophe, and had established Pharaoh on his throne, had faded, and in its place there was a growing sense of national unease on account of the all-too-visibly-strong alien race living in the midst of Egypt.

The new Pharaoh had become fearful of the Children of Israel. His fear had grown as the descendants of Jacob had increased in number. The fear was, at least in his own mind, quite rational: the numerous Israelites might act as a fifth column, join with a foreign power, and sweep him and his people away.

The problem was obvious and the solution simple. Pharaoh gave orders that the birth of a girl should be ignored but that all boys born to Hebrew parents must be seized and thrown into the Nile. When the life of a child is threatened by an incurable disease we cannot help but feel something of the parents' burden, but when the life of a child is threatened by the powers of the state, arising out of the fears of those who hold power without accountability, we feel not only the sorrow of impending death but of helpless frustration. Amram and his pregnant wife Jochebed, living as aliens in a foreign land, might have been forgiven for feeling distressed and perplexed.

Perhaps they had prayed that they might be spared the cruel fate of seeing their soon-to-be-born child being ripped from their arms and mercilessly put to death by the powers that be. If only God would give them another baby girl—a sister for Miriam! For them, too, the problem was obvious and the solution simple. As the months passed and the child grew within her womb, Jochebed, it might reasonably be supposed, grew more and more anxious as to the future. If she had a son, how long would she have him for?

The day arrived and Jochebed was delivered of a child. Joy no doubt that she had a healthy child! Joy no doubt that she could present her husband Amram with another son! But what anxious thoughts must have intermingled with the delight, that some officer of the state would pluck him from her breast and cast him into the waters of the Nile?

For three months she hid him, anxious that some overly zealous soldier might make too close an inspection. How often would she have prayed! How earnestly would Amram and Jochebed have knelt down beside their infant son and pleaded with the Lord to protect their little baby boy! It does not require great imagination; just a little empathy. If you are a parent, or can at least place yourself in their circumstances, how might you have prayed? I think I would have prayed for the Lord's protection: that my little son would not cry out at the wrong moment and draw attention to himself; that any passing soldier would be too busy or too careless to make a close inquiry; that those who knew would keep the secret. Anxious days and troubled nights were doubtless spent wondering if it might please the Lord to spare the life of the little child.

Three months passed until Jochebed could conceal him no longer. Taking a basket she daubed it with bitumen and pitch so that it would be watertight and float. Carefully and tenderly she placed her little boy into the basket. Pharaoh had ordered that male children should be cast into the river, and that was what she did! Nearby she arranged for Miriam to watch over him. Perhaps she herself could not bear to watch. It would be hard to imagine placing your infant child in a wicker basket and placing him in the water—how unimaginably painful to do so, knowing that if the currents did not sweep him away, at any moment his life might be taken by a passing official. A last word of charge to Miriam. A last word of prayer committing her little boy to the Lord. Who can doubt that as she turned from the river her eyes were filled with tears, her breath shortened, her pulse racing?

How would the Lord answer this mother's prayers? Prayers for safety and protection. 'Protect him from all harm!'

In God's providence, it was at this time that Pharaoh's daughter with her attendants came down to the Nile to bathe. Evidently, either she or one of her servants saw the basket in the water and it aroused her curiosity. The basket was brought near for closer inspection. Taking away the swaddling cloths she saw a three-month-old child. The child began to cry. What was it about the child? Perhaps the sheer helplessness of an infant adrift on the river. An infant startled by a stranger and bereft of the familiar face and comforting voice of a nursing mother, may have brought forth tears that touched the heart of a princess, even though this was so obviously a Hebrew child. Whatever the response, it was sufficiently tender to encourage Miriam to come out of her hiding place and offer to find someone to nurse the child for the princess.

Though we ought not to be, we are astonished at all that now unfolds. Jochebed had arisen that morning with a particularly heavy heart as she contemplated making a basket for her little boy and placing it in the river. By the time the sun had set she found herself in the employment of the royal household being paid to nurse her own son.

Pharaoh out of fear had given a cruel order for the death of male infants. A mother had pleaded for her son's life. But *God is always better than we can imagine*.

The princess named the little boy Moses and he was brought up at Pharaoh's court. He received the finest education available and was tutored in the ways of the kings of Egypt. He was able to speak the language of politics and diplomacy, and was intimately acquainted with the etiquette that surrounds every royal throne. He was raised knowing the personalities and practicalities of everyday life in the corridors of power. He was raised as one used to exercising authority and leadership.

A mother's prayer had been answered exceedingly abundantly beyond what she could ask or even imagine.

For further reflection:

1. How much do we take into consideration the greatness of God when we pray?

2. How should we pray when we think of who God is?

3. Should we complain if God does not answer exactly as we have prayed?

Meditation 10

The Gospel in the Law: The Eighth Commandment

You shall not steal. — Exodus 20:15.

I think I paid around £80 for my first car. Of course, that was more than forty years ago. Looking back I am not entirely convinced that it was worth that much even in today's money. My second one cost me less, but didn't last much longer. The third was a comfortable car but it too was really on loan from the scrap yard. By the time I got to my fourth I was able to trade up to a car that actually looked as though it would make it to the petrol station.

To say that I was vexed when I went out one morning to find someone had broken into that car and stolen the radio, would be an understatement. If having someone whipped through the streets while rotting vegetation was hurled in his direction had been an option, I think I would have been almost content—once he had replaced my radio and repaired the damage to my car, of course. It's not really terribly surprising that when we are the ones who have sustained damage we desire the full weight of the law to be applied.

On the other hand, I have to confess that a couple of years ago, I did get pulled over by the police. The country road on which I was driving had ended at the edge of town, and I hadn't seen the speed limit sign. The policeman walked up to my window and asked me what my reason was for going so fast. No doubt he had heard them all: a dying grandmother, a friend in the Emergency Room, a faulty accelerator. I am neither bright nor quick enough to think of some excuse he had not heard, quite aside from any violation of the ninth commandment that such an excuse would entail.

'No excuse!' I said, 'It's my responsibility as the driver to be looking for the road signs and I can't have been paying sufficient attention.'

Maybe it was because I was driving a rental car and my accent indicated I was from way out of town, that the officer let me off. Or, maybe it was because he just wasn't used to hearing a driver admit that he was in the wrong. Whatever the reason, I was very glad that he did not deal with me as I deserved. My attitude was the polar opposite of what it had been the morning I found that someone had broken the window of my car and stolen the radio. Then I wanted the full weight of the law to be exercised. But when I was the culprit, what I wanted was leniency. I was glad when the policeman let me off with a warning.

For most folk, the different reactions need no further explanation. When someone has harmed me or mine, I want justice. When I am in the wrong I want mercy. Either way the law is the great rock which we either want to fall on someone else or hope it doesn't fall on us. What we are not going to have is a really warm affection towards it. The law is the law and it is there to punish wrongdoers, but I don't have much in the way of affection towards it.

So that's what makes David's attitude so very striking. He was a man who not only said he *loved* the law, but he *made it his meditation day and night*. Every child who has been through Sunday School will know that the chapter with the most verses in the Bible is Psalm 119. It has 176 verses, each one of which, with one or two exceptions, makes mention of the law in some form or another. If you are looking at a translation of the original Hebrew text, you may see above each section of eight verses of the psalm a Hebrew letter of the alphabet. Each verse in that section begins with a word that starts with that particular letter. The author went to a great deal of trouble to write this psalm in praise of the law of God.

The congregation the Lord has called me to serve is blessed with men who are highly skilled in the construction trade, but I have yet to hear one say, 'Oh, how I love the building code! It is my meditation all the day.' Not even close! So why does David have this love affair with the law? And, should his attitude be ours?

Let me make a bold statement: If you don't love the law of God it is because you don't understand it. That is a bit of a challenge to probably many Christians who tend to make law the opposite of grace. In this generation it seems that few preachers make much of the 'law' and prefer instead to emphasize the 'gospel.' So perhaps you think that the emphasis should be for us to tell folks what 'sinners' they are so that they should know how great the Saviour is. Well, that is certainly true; for unless we know what a catastrophe sin is in our lives, then we will never truly know how good God is in saving us from it, or indeed, just how much God has done for us in Christ. But that will still put law in opposition to grace, and will not help us understand the reasons why David loved the law so much.

There are some basic principles in opening up the law which, when applied, start to crack open to us just why someone could love the law as much as David did. I hope that you, with me, will begin to love God's law too.

Let us take the law that says we should not steal—the eighth commandment. Perhaps, by God's grace you were brought up in a Christian home and attended a church where the law was regularly read. You may, in fact, be able to recite the Ten Commandments, if not word for word at least with sufficient understanding to be able to give them in the right order.

I went to Sunday School too. In fact I went to a second one in the afternoon each Lord's day. Perhaps my mother thought I was in need of some remedial education, but that's another story. I can remember Sunday School teachers going through the Ten Commandments and seeking to make application to their young charges. Taking the Lord's name in vain was linked to hitting your thumb with a hammer and letting out an oath. The construction men in my congregation are far too skilled for that ever to happen, while I am not to be trusted with a hammer in any case. It is, therefore, not a realistic scenario in my experience. But the point was made.

The problem with such illustrations is that they teach us to regard the law in a superficial manner. We make our applications, convince ourselves that we have a handle on what it has to say, and move on without further reflection.

If that were all there were to it, then we have largely a list of what not to do. But we have surely come to expect more from God and his word. When, for example, we think of stealing, we can understand that God is prohibiting taking what does not belong to us. But the law has a positive application too. In application of this commandment Paul wrote to the church in Ephesus: 'Let the thief no longer steal, but rather let him labour, doing honest work with his own hands, so that he may have something to share with anyone in need' (Eph. 4:28).

Do you see what Paul is saying? The thief is no longer to steal. That's a straight forward and direct application of the eighth commandment. But then he goes on to make a further application. Rather than stealing he is to work, and the reason given is that he should not only provide for himself but that he should have something to share with anyone in need.

In the commandments then, we not only have a negative but a positive application too.

Jesus had to combat a superficial view of the command-ments in the thinking of the Pharisees. They were 'experts' in the law. But in their thinking it seemed as if avoiding the prohibited action was all that the commandment required. Your heart could be a cesspool of evil thoughts, but so long as you hadn't actually committed the act all was well. No wonder the Lord said that the hypocritical Pharisees were like whitened sepulchres: on the outside pristine but on the inside filled with the deathly corrup-tion. It is not just the outside that needs to be guarded and kept clean, but the heart itself, the well-spring of all our actions.

The most important aspect for a true understanding of the law of God is to see it as a reflection of God's own character. God is telling us about himself in each of the Ten Commandments. Take the seventh commandment against committing adultery. Another way of saying that someone has committed adultery is to say that he or she has been unfaithful. Actually if you are reading through the Old Testament, the term 'adultery' is used with refer-ence to the Children of Israel far more frequently than it is of the relationship between a man and a woman. God's own people were unfaithful to him and 'committed adultery' with foreign gods.

Now this starts to open up how David could love God's law so much. In the law God was not only telling his people that they should not commit adultery, but that they should be faithful to their marriage partner. He was telling them something else—something that would comfort their souls. He was telling them that it was his nature to be faithful. He is not going to command us to be faithful while being unfaithful himself. We are commanded to be holy *as he is holy*, and he tells us how we can do just that. As John Donne put it in *The Progress of the Soul*, 'Would God (disputes the curious rebel) make a law, and would not have it kept?'

God is telling us about himself in the Ten Commandments. We are expecting him to reveal great things about himself. We come primed in anticipation that *he is always better than we can imagine*. So let us make application of that principle to the eighth commandment.

God tells us not to steal. That means we should not take what does not belong to us. The opposite is also contained in that commandment, which would be that we are to take that which does belong to us and use it for the help of someone who has need.

But because God is always better than we can imagine, and God is telling us about himself, we can make application of this commandment to God himself. God will not steal from us. He will not take from us what does not belong to him. On the contrary, he takes what does belong to him and uses it to bless those who are in need.

There is a well known verse which is really a commentary on the eighth commandment. Here it is: 'For God so loved the world, that he gave his only Son, that whoever believes in him should not perish but have eternal life' (John 3:16). Oh, how I love your law! It is my meditation all the night!

For further reflection:

1. What do the Ten Commandments teach you about the character of God?

2. How was it possible for David to love the law of God so much?

3. How can you come to love God's law?

Meditation 11

When God Could Bear It No Longer

And the people of Israel cried out to the LORD, saying, 'We have sinned against you, because we have forsaken our God and have served the Baals.' And the LORD said to the people of Israel, "Did I not save you from the Egyptians and from the Amorites, from the Ammonites and from the Philistines? The Sidonians also, and the Amalekites and the Maonites oppressed you, and you cried out to me, and I saved you out of their hand. Yet you have forsaken me and served other gods; therefore I will save you no more. Go and cry out to the gods whom you have chosen; let them save you in the time of your distress.' And the people of Israel said to the LORD, 'We have sinned; do to us whatever seems good to you. Only please deliver us this day.' So they put away the foreign gods from among them and served the LORD, and he became impatient over the misery of Israel. Then the Ammonites were called to arms, and they encamped in Gilead. And the people of Israel came together, and they

> encamped at Mizpah. And the people, the lead-
> ers of Gilead, said one to another, 'Who is the
> man who will begin to fight against the Ammo-
> nites? He shall be head over all the inhabitants of
> Gilead.'—Judges 10:10-18.

The Book of Judges makes for very unhappy reading. It begins with the death of Joshua and after that the cycle of blessing, judgment, repentance, blessing, etc., is pretty remorseless. The very rhythm of Israel's spiritual life is depressing in itself. Israel has not proved radical in its uprooting of the nations they were commanded to remove. Now before we start feeling sorry for these pagan peoples, we should remember that they were wicked, and that the Lord was exercising his justice in bringing judgment upon them. They were not peaceable and gentle folk, quietly minding their own business when the Israelites wandered over the horizon in a frenzy of destruction.

These were people who worshipped gods who demanded that their infants be burned to death. They were most definitely not 'noble savages' stoically providing for their families in a hostile environment. But in spite of the task set before the Children of Israel both to bring judgment on godless nations and to take possession of the land God had given them, the Israelites had—not to put too fine a point on it—taken the easy option. Much easier by far to work out a degree of accommodation with the local residents, than do the hard work of actually driving them out. Really, is it so very different today? What about us? When God calls us to exercise a radical separation from the godlessness of this world, are we swift to root the world out of us, or is our first inclination to make concessions and accommodations, so that we can get on with living in friendship with the world? Well does the writer to the Hebrews speak of the sin 'which clings so closely' (Heb. 12:1). Just ask anyone from Mississippi. It was my privilege to pastor there for a while. Driving into Jackson one could often see on both sides of the road a plant that had been introduced from Japan. It was called kudzu. Now kudzu had done a pretty good job of colonizing any spare ground. For those not familiar with kudzu, picture a sort of ivy that grows so very quickly. It will cover everything before long. It grows across the ground, up the telegraph pole, along the wires and everywhere else. It is the sort of stuff the science-fiction horror movies are made of. But what a picture of sin; the 'sin which clings so easily.' Stand too long in any one place in Mississippi, and you might be entangled in kudzu yourself.

By contrast what we are called on to do is take up the machete of the word of God and cut away at sin. And that's precisely what the Children of Israel did not do. The description of Scripture is rather telling. 'When Israel grew strong, they put the Canaanites to forced labor, but did not drive them out completely' (Judg. 1:28). Strange, isn't it how we can see precisely where other people go wrong, but don't see it in ourselves. Though the Children of Israel were strong and therefore had the opportunity to drive out the Canaanites, they preferred a policy of accommodation. It is not that we can't see the logic. 'Hey, instead of driving out the Canaanites, they can serve us!' The Israelites are spared the effort and they get a bunch of folk to do their bidding. Isn't that a win-win situation for the Children of Israel?

Well, not according to the angel of the Lord. Those Canaanites were going to be thorns in the sides of the Israelites, and their gods were going to be snares to them. And so it proved to be.

It is not long before we are reading that the Israelites did evil in the eyes of the Lord. They forgot the Lord their God. They served the Baals and Ashtoreths. The people of God cried out to the Lord, and he graciously raised up a deliverer in the form of Othniel. Othniel died and once again the Israelites did evil in the sight of the Lord. God handed them over to the Moabites who oppressed them until they cried out for a deliverer. Then God raised up Ehud. Ehud died and the Israelites once again did evil in the eyes of the Lord so he gave them over to the king of Canaan. Yes, that's right—the very people the Israelites thought they could harness for their own ends. But the people of God were not so strong now, and the king of Canaan had the Israelites as his servants. The response of the children of Israel? They cried out to the Lord and the Lord raised up Deborah. Deborah is not long off the scene when again the Israelites did evil in the eyes of the Lord. This time it was the Midianites who were the instruments of God's judgment on his own people. Of course, the people cried out to the Lord, and the Lord raised up Gideon.

The dreadful inevitability of the cycle of events is depressing. 'As soon as Gideon died, the people of Israel turned again and whored after the Baals' (Judg. 8:33). And so it continues down to Jephthah, the judge who promised to offer to God whatever came out of the door of his house to meet him on his return, if God would give the Ammonites into his hand.

Now this is not the time or place to get caught up in the question of whether or not Jephthah ultimately offered up his daughter as a burnt offering or not. The sheer folly of the vow is staggering. It didn't occur to him that the 'whatever' would turn out to be a 'whoever'! A wife, a child, a servant. So, perhaps he was thinking his dog would come rushing out to meet him. Did the ancient Israelite keep their dogs in the house? I don't know, but even if we grant that, why was Jephthah offering God his dog? 'Lord, if you deliver the Ammonites into my hand and free Israel from the curse of oppression, I will sacrifice my cocker spaniel as a burnt offering'! That leaves me rather unimpressed. However you read the account, the more you think about it, the more perplexing and fraught with difficulties it becomes.

But that may be the point.

There was no king in Israel in those days and everyone did what was right in his own eyes. Israel was living in a time of spiritual and moral anarchy. It wasn't just that they were addicted to following the gods of the nations they were supposed to have removed from the land, but when the oppression of evil rose to the level of being unbearable, they hardly knew the way back. Even the response had become formulaic; 'We have sinned against you, because we have forsaken our God and have served the Baals' (Judg. 10:10). It is almost as though their crying out were just part of the natural cycle; the Israelites sinned by worshipping false gods, God punished them with oppression, the Israelites cried out, and then God raised up a deliverer to rescue them. When the deliverer died the cycle would start all over again. The Israelites had been doing that for generations already. But this time was different. Repentance is not just the outward form of words. It was time for them to 'rend their hearts and not their garments' (cf. Joel 2:13).

It is interesting to note that it is only after God declines to come to their aid that the Children of Israel put away their foreign gods. Well, God is gracious and we anticipate that he will indeed come to their rescue once more. But tucked away in Judges chapter 10 is a glimpse of a *God who is always better than we can imagine*.

You see, we might be tempted to look at the repentance of the Israelites as being rather superficial to begin with. Once they demonstrated a bit more seriousness in their repentance, God relented and came to their rescue. So is that how it works? Is our repentance the ground or basis for God's intervention? To be sure, without repentance God will not intervene, but the text gives it away: 'and he became impatient over the misery of

Israel' (10:16). Israel's misery grieved him until he could bear it no longer.

I think we are all hard-wired to favour justification by works. 'Is there not something that I can do that will in some way earn my salvation? Surely my faith God rewards with salvation. I have to repent, and then God rewards that repentance with salvation.'

Martin Luther thought he might be able get into heaven by 'punishment beatings.' And so he would whip himself mercilessly in the hope that God would forgive him his sins. In doing so he was following the medieval practice of the 'flagellants' who would lash themselves until the blood ran down their backs. Though such self-mutilation is now rare in the Western world, its underlying cause is ever present within our hearts. We all-too-easily believe that God is not altogether willing to forgive our sins. But this text gives the lie to that. What moved God was not the mixed-up theology and less than thoroughgoing repentance of the Israelites. No, the reason for God show-ing grace to them was to be found in God himself. 'He became impatient over the misery of Israel.'

I can offer you, dear reader, no hope of salvation, if you do not repent. But I do not wish the enemy of your soul to snatch away your hope, to leave you wondering whether you have repented sufficiently to merit salva-tion. Your confidence must rest wholly on a *God who is always better than you can imagine*. The next time the enemy tempts you to despair that perhaps you have not repented enough, think on this: the Saviour went more willingly to the cross for his people than you go to the throne of grace for forgiveness. Our confidence rests in him and in him alone.

For further reflection:

1. Is your repentance before God just a matter of routine?

2. Where does our confidence in God's willingness to forgive lie?

3. How willing is God to forgive you your sins?

Meditation 12

Hannah Asked for a Son

After they had eaten and drunk in Shiloh, Hannah rose. Now Eli the priest was sitting on the seat beside the doorpost of the temple of the LORD. She was deeply distressed and prayed to the LORD and wept bitterly. And she vowed a vow and said, 'O LORD of hosts, if you will indeed look on the affliction of your servant and remember me and not forget your servant, but will give to your servant a son, then I will give him to the LORD all the days of his life, and no razor shall touch his head.' As she continued praying before the LORD, Eli observed her mouth. Hannah was speaking in her heart; only her lips moved, and her voice was not heard. Therefore Eli took her to be a drunken woman. And Eli said to her, 'How long will you go on being drunk? Put away your wine from you.' But Hannah answered, 'No, my lord, I am a woman troubled in spirit. I have drunk neither wine nor strong drink, but I have been pouring out my soul before the LORD. Do not regard your servant as a worthless woman, for all along I have been speaking out of my great anxiety and vexation.' Then Eli answered, 'Go in peace, and the God of Israel grant your petition that you have made to him.' And she said, 'Let your servant find favor in your eyes.' Then the woman went her way and ate, and her face was no longer sad.—1 Samuel 1:9-18.

Is there a pain endured by a couple worse than that of longing for a child which God sovereignly withholds? Perhaps the only sorrow that would surpass it is the sorrow of losing a child. By the mercy of God, few of us experience such an agony of soul firsthand, but perhaps most of us have observed the distress in others whom we love and hold dear. A child is presented for baptism and the family and congregation rejoice, and rightly so. But there in our midst is the childless couple who smile with genuine gladness at the Lord's blessing on others, while their eyes tell you just how much they long for the day when they might present a child of their own for baptism.

Childlessness features often in Scripture. Abraham and Sarah waited a long time for Isaac. Isaac and Rebecca waited a long time for Esau and Jacob. Jacob and Rachel waited a long time for Joseph. Considering that fruitfulness was an integral part of God's promise to Abraham and his descendants, childlessness features surprisingly frequently.

And that brings us to Hannah and her longing for a child. Hannah was married to Elkanah. Now Elkanah had two wives, the other being Peninnah. Peninnah was blessed with children but Hannah was not. Peninnah does not appear to have been very gracious in her dealings with Hannah. I doubt if the taunts were obvious. They were probably the kind of verbal jabs that would strike between the ribs and cut straight to the heart: 'I was up all night with Elkanah Jr. I wish I could get a night's uninterrupted sleep. But he does need to be fed and changed regularly...' We have all experience of that sort of thing. It is nothing you can really respond to. In this case it was not an outright mentioning of Hannah's childless condition, but a constant drawing of attention to the responsibilities of motherhood—the unspoken subtext being that Peninnah has to deal with it while Hannah does not.

Now I have to admit that this is somewhat speculative but it is a reasonable inference from the text. Elkanah was a kindly and considerate man who was sensitive to Hannah's condition, and he doesn't come across as the sort of man who would sit idly by while Peninnah was verbally abusing Hannah. Peninnah's actions were more subtle than that. Worse still, they were not isolated incidents but part of every-day life for Hannah. And the taunting got even worse when the devout Elkanah took his family on their regular visits to Shiloh to worship the Lord. Perhaps it was the absence of the usual domestic routine that afforded more opportunities for Peninnah to provoke Hannah. Perhaps it was the opportunity to remind Hannah that others had been given the blessing of the Lord that she so much desired. But whatever the reason the outcome was the same. Poor Hannah was thoroughly upset and miserable. Elkanah did his best to make up for it by giving her a double helping of food at mealtimes. One wonders if that just stirred Peninnah up still more out of jealousy for her husband's attention.

If he could be somewhat inept in his actions, he could also make a mess of his personal interactions. 'Don't I mean more to you than ten sons?' The question is just all wrong, though well intentioned and lovingly meant. It came from a tender heart. But it was still all wrong. It seems that Hannah was really carrying the burden on her own. Peninnah had no interest in lightening her load. Indeed she was part of the burden. Elkanah was well intentioned but didn't appear really to understand, or he would not have asked such a question. We are not surprised, then, when it is Hannah who enters the place of worship on her own to pray.

You can picture her eyes filling up as she rises from the table, biting her lip to hold in the raw emotion, and holding the folds of her garment to allow her feet to carry her quickly to a quiet spot to pour out her heart before the Lord. Arriving at the place of worship and possibly thinking that she was alone and unobserved, the fountains of her eyes burst open as the sorrow of her heart gushes forth. She is in God's presence and does not need to hide the sorrow of her heart. Though she made no sound, her lips moved as she petitioned God. She prayed for a son. The prayer was not long and complicated, but simple and straightforward. If the Lord would remember her and give her a son, she would give him back to the Lord, never allowing a razor to be used on his head. Like Samson, he would be a Nazarite.

At this point you might think that poor Hannah has enough to cope with; but rising out of the shadows comes Eli. He was God's man, and in charge of the place of worship. He suspected Hannah to be drunk. Well, it just wouldn't be right to have some drunken woman making a mockery of the place of worship, so he gives her a good telling off. (Those who are called to be ministers of God don't always get it right, do they? They are men with feet of clay, and on this occasion both Eli's feet of clay were inserted into his mouth!) Alas, in the place where Hannah should have found relief from her burden, it seems as if Eli's words have only added to her affliction.

Eli was wrong in his assessment of the situation. Hannah denied his allegation and then explained the reason for her great sorrow. It may have been out of embarrassment at his mistake, but he responded by expressing the hope that God would grant her petition. In any case, Hannah was encouraged by his words, dried her eyes, and had something to eat. Her spirit was lifted. Sometimes it really doesn't take much. A word spoken in season can bring a surprisingly liberal dose of encouragement. We would do well to remember the example of Hannah when we are tempted to rush away without waiting for a word of encouragement. Old Eli bungled the first point of contact but God still used him to bless the troubled heart of Hannah.

Those who have more than a passing knowledge of

Scripture will recognize that Hannah was the mother of Samuel, one of the greatest of Old Testament characters. God answered her prayer and Samuel served the Lord faithfully all the days of his long life. God answered her prayer in that respect abundantly. But I think there is something more in Hannah's story.

Having received Samuel as a gift from the Lord, she gives him back as soon as he was weaned. And when was that? Though some cultures have longer weaning times than others, it seems likely that Samuel was around four years old when Hannah fulfilled her promise to give him back to the Lord.

I began by suggesting that the only sorrow which might surpass that of being without a longed-for child, is losing a child. Hannah trusted the Lord, and having laid her request before him, looked to him to grant her heart's desire. But then having granted her heart's desire, Hannah lays the most precious gift she has on the altar of her love for God. She withholds nothing from him, not even her dearly beloved little boy 'Samuel' whom she 'asked of the Lord.' As soon as he has been weaned she takes the little fellow by the hand and places that little hand in the hand of Eli.

Scripture then records Hannah's prayer. The woman who wanted nothing so much as to be a mother has weaned the child and now hands him to Eli with the words 'My heart exults in the LORD.' The one who gives to the Lord will losing nothing by doing so.

She went on to declare her trust in God:

> There is none holy like the LORD;
>> there is none besides you;
>> there is no rock like our God.

Surely Hannah was now impervious to every taunt of Peninnah.

For further reflection:

1. Is there any sorrow that you cannot bring to the Lord?

2. Did the delay in answering Hannah's prayer make the gift of Samuel greater or lesser?

3. What was Hannah's final circumstance?

Meditation 13

The House of David Blessed Forever

Then King David went in and sat before the Lord
and said, 'Who am I, O Lord God, and what is
my house, that you have brought me thus far?
And this was a small thing in your eyes, O God.
You have also spoken of your servant's house for
a great while to come, and have shown me future
generations, O Lord God! And what more can
David say to you for honouring your servant?
For you know your servant. For your servant's
sake, O Lord, and according to your own heart,
you have done all this greatness, in making
known all these great things. There is none like
you, O Lord, and there is no God besides you,
according to all that we have heard with our
ears. And who is like your people Israel, the one
nation on earth whom God went to redeem to
be his people, making for yourself a name for
great and awesome things, in driving out nations
before your people whom you redeemed from
Egypt? And you made your people Israel to be
your people forever, and you, O Lord, became

their God. And now, O Lord, let the word that you have spoken concerning your servant and concerning his house be established forever, and do as you have spoken, and your name will be established and magnified forever, saying, "The Lord of hosts, the God of Israel, is Israel's God," and the house of your servant David will be established before you. For you, my God, have revealed to your servant that you will build a house for him. Therefore your servant has found courage to pray before you. And now, O Lord, you are God, and you have promised this good thing to your servant. Now you have been pleased to bless the house of your servant, that it may continue forever before you, for it is you, O Lord, who have blessed, and it is blessed forever.'

— 1 Chronicles 17:16-27.

It wasn't easy for David. He may have been the man after God's own heart but that didn't mean everything was handed to him on a plate. When we are first introduced to him, Samuel has come to anoint a son of Jesse to be king. Jesse presents his sons; the oldest, Eliab, first as we would expect in that culture. Samuel looked at the strong young man and at his height and was sure this had to be the one. The Lord has to point out to Samuel that it is not physical strength that he is looking for but spiritual. The Lord can use the most unlikely material for his glory. That is a great comfort for me and, I trust, a great comfort for you too!

So Eliab was not the one to be anointed by Samuel. Who's next, Abinadab? No, not him either. Shimea? No, not him. Nethanel? No, try again. Raddai? No, I'm afraid not. Jesse was running out of sons to present to Samuel. Ozem? No, not him. Has Jesse got no other sons? Well, there is one more, just a boy really, out in the fields with the sheep. Jesse hadn't even thought to send for him. But Samuel insists: 'We'll not sit down until he is here!' So a messenger was sent out into fields near Bethlehem to the shepherds who were keeping watch over the sheep. (Centuries later another generation of shepherds would rush into Bethlehem from the same fields to see 'great David's Greater Son,' but that's another story.)

David came at his father's bidding, and could not have realized the least part of what was going to happen. In the presence of his father and brothers, Samuel, the revered prophet of God, anointed him, no doubt to their and his great astonishment.

Samuel returned to Ramah. Jesse and his sons, including David, went back to doing whatever they were doing before Samuel had come to town to offer a sacrifice. Anointing David with oil seems not to have had much effect on the days that followed—at least not to the outward eye. But the statement is unmistakable that just as the Lord looks upon the inward heart and not the outward physique, so Scripture tells us directly what we could not see for ourselves, that the Spirit of the Lord came upon David in power.

Scripture then shifts our focus to Saul whom the Lord has rejected, and from whom the Spirit of the Lord has departed. He is tormented. Well, 'music hath charms to soothe a savage breast,' and David is recommended to Saul as someone who is skilled in playing the harp. It seems that David's playing did indeed having a calming influence on Saul. It was not, though, an obvious step towards the throne.

The next encounter with the boy who would be king, was when Goliath challenged the armies of the Children of Israel. You can't help but think that war was a more leisurely pursuit in those days. Goliath came out every day for forty days to insult God and his people. And for forty days the people of God listened and did nothing. It is during this period that David comes to bring supplies to his brothers who served in Saul's army. When Goliath steps out again to insult God and his people, the Israelites, who are too close for comfort, flee in fear. David's response is just the opposite: 'Who is this uncircumcised Philistine that he should defy the armies of the living God?'

David not only overcame Goliath but everyone else who came against him. The young women made up their songs, 'Saul has slain his thousands, and David his tens of thousands!' That went down well with everyone—everyone except Saul, that is. A nobler spirit might have rejoiced in David's success but Saul didn't like the comparison. Can you sympathize with Saul? As others have observed, it's not enough to succeed, others must fail! If we are kept from such a bitter view of life, have we been granted sufficient grace to rejoice, and truly so, when others succeed where we have failed? That's a tough one. Saul had clearly not mastered that grace. On more than one occasion he tried to pin David to the wall with a spear, and spent no little time and energy in pursuing him so that he could destroy him.

For David's part, he had to hide from Saul, and though granted a couple of opportunities to put an end to Saul's life, he refrained from doing so. Perhaps he didn't do so because regicide was not a good way to begin a reign. It might encourage others to seize power by the same means. But, as Scripture indicates, David genuinely did not wish to take up arms against the one whom God had anointed to be king. He was always swift to bring judgment on those who did.

God's training period for David proved to be long and hard. He was anointed when still so young that no one—not even his brothers or father—considered him a serious candidate for the crown.

When David prayed that his life might be spared, it was not whining self-pity but an honest assessment of just how precarious his life was. There were plenty who would have been quite happy to win Saul's favour by bringing him David's head.

Years later, in calmer days, David reflected God's answer to prayer in Psalm 21. God had granted him victories. He says, 'you meet him with rich blessings; you set a crown of fine gold upon his head. He asked life of you; you gave it to him, length of days, forever and ever' (Psa. 21:3, 4).

It doesn't take much imagination to understand why David would be praying for life when he was taking refuge in a remote cave with Saul and his army in hot pursuit of him. David recognizes that God indeed gave him life; he did not only spare his life on that particular occasion, but he was to give him much more besides. David had asked for life and *God, who is always better than we can imagine*, gave him long life. And more, he gave him eternal life.

David seemed to recognize that there was more to God's promise of life. His devotion to the Lord meant he longed to see the ark of the covenant brought into his capital city. When this was accomplished he went in and sat before the Lord. His prayer is full of wonder at God's astounding grace. 'Who am I, and what is my family, that you have brought me this far?' God's goodness and grace to him makes him bold in prayer: 'And now, O Lord, let the word that you have spoken concerning your servant and concerning his house be established forever.'

One wonders what David had in mind. Probably that a son of his would rule after him, and his son should continue, and so on through the generations; a royal dynasty that would stand the test of time. But could he possibly have conceived what God had planned? That the long-awaited Messiah, God in flesh, would be his descendant, and that his throne truly would last not just for time but for eternity! The throne of Solomon, his son, was the wonder of its age; its glory far surpassed that of David's; but how much more glorious shall be the reign of the one who is 'greater than Solomon'?

One wonders if David recognized the eternal dimensions of his prayer when the ark of God was brought into Jerusalem: 'Now you have been pleased to bless the house of your servant, that it may continue forever before you, for it is you, O LORD, who have blessed, and it is blessed forever.'

Though with the understanding and the revelation of the New Testament we might possess a great appreciation of the answering of that prayer, truly as God is always better than we can imagine, the fullness of God's answer will only begin to be known in eternity.

For further reflection:

1. Do you genuinely rejoice at the success of others?

2. How much greater was the throne of Solomon than David's?

3. How much greater still shall be the throne of great David's Greater Son?

Meditation 14

Is It Too Late to Turn Back?

> They say, If a man put away his wife, and she
> go from him, and become another man's, shall
> he return unto her again? shall not that land be
> greatly polluted? but thou hast played the harlot
> with many lovers; yet return again to me, saith
> the LORD.—Jeremiah 3:1 (KJV).

Have you committed the unpardonable sin? It has been
some time since I have had to speak pastorally to someone who feared that he or she was beyond the reach of
God's forgiveness. That may be a sign of the times. Everyone feels so good about himself or herself that it never
crosses the mind that God would have any reason to be
remotely displeased with him or her. It hasn't always been
that way. The best known sermon of Jonathan Edwards,
'Sinners in the hands of an angry God,' is at some pains
to point out that our lives hang by a thread and that it is
a dreadful thing to fall into the hands of an angry God.
I suspect that the academic circles in which such a text
might still be handled regard such a thought as at best
rather quaint and at worst even abusive of its hearers.

And yet God used that sermon quite remarkably in the Great Awakening of the eighteenth century. Men and women during those days when the Spirit of God was poured out from heaven, clung to pillars in the church for fear they would fall into hell.

Those days may be gone for now. By the grace of God I hope that they have not gone for good, and I pray that the Lord would awaken the consciences of men and women to the power of his truth through a fresh outpouring of his Spirit.

But what would it take for the Western nations in particular to be brought to their senses? We can, at the very least, be assured that God does not visit any judgment upon a nation more than it deserves, and if his purpose is to bring a people back to himself, he will not add one ounce of affliction more than is necessary to accomplish the task. If it be the former then let us praise God for his justice, and if the latter, for his mercy.

These are sobering thoughts. The days of Jeremiah were sobering too, for the Lord was visiting Israel with his judgment because the nation had strayed so very far from him. Famine afflicted everyone from the highest to the lowest. When God's prophet was arrested and imprisoned, the Scriptures simply record that he was given a loaf a day until the bread ran out. It is not a pleasant scene to contemplate: famine so severe that men dropped from want of food in the streets, families reduced to eating what previously they would not have considered touching, refined folks with dainty manners and an educated palate foraging for scraps wherever they might be found.

Though it might not have been recognized by many, and certainly not by king Zedekiah, there was a glimmer of hope. There was a difference in the land between the days of Elijah when the Lord closed the heavens for three and a half years which brought great distress on the land. Can you think of what that difference was?

In Elijah's day, the prophet himself was hidden. The famine was not one of food and water only. The real famine in the land in those days was the withholding of the preaching of the word of God. Perhaps as we consider the state of Western nations and perceive the judgment of God resting on us, it may encourage us to recognize that the Lord has not utterly removed faithful men from the pulpit. Thank God there are still those who faithfully preach and teach the gospel of Jesus Christ.

In Jeremiah's day, even when the nation was under God's judgment, with Nebuchadnezzar king of Babylon about to conquer the land and ransack the city of Jerusalem, God's word was still being preached by the prophet he had raised up and set apart for that sacred task.

It is in such a context that Jeremiah preaches on a most striking theme. He speaks of a woman who wilfully leaves her own husband. Now here is something of which we should be aware: though adultery is mentioned in Scripture, more often than not the adultery of which the Bible speaks is the adultery committed by the Children of Israel in their unfaithfulness to God. So what is Jeremiah saying? God is the faithful husband who has treated his bride with gentleness, love, care, and indeed all the other qualities that are associated with an ideal husband. In return the bride has gone off with another man. Well, actually, not just another man, with other men!

In such circumstances, should the husband take her back? Jeremiah says plainly that to do so would pollute the land. No doubt he is reflecting on Deuteronomy 24:4 in his response: 'then her former husband, who sent her away, may not take her again to be his wife, after she has been defiled, for that is an abomination before the LORD.' A message from the God who will 'by no means clear the guilty' brings little comfort.

So how does a righteous God maintain his justice, and yet pardon the guilty?

God uses the same picture elsewhere in Scripture with another prophet, Hosea. He was told to marry a prostitute. Even after the marriage had taken place she continued to be unfaithful to the man of God. It really is quite a heart-breaking story, and it is meant to be.

When Gomer, Hosea's wife, was young and pretty she found it easy enough to turn heads. She could have the pick of any man she desired, and apparently she often did. But there is a price to be paid for living in an ungodly way, and the flower of youth fades so quickly. No longer the young and attractive girl who turned the heads of all the young men, she is now a not so young and a not so attractive woman, and those who had seemingly been so attracted were now more and more repelled by her.

Those charms which had secured her a ready income and so many fine things, were not so charming. The trinkets she had bought, or which had been bought for her, had to be sold to pay the rent. As time passed they were soon all gone. She was anything but a pretty sight. Her last option was to sell herself as a slave.

Now come with me in your imagination to that slave market. Such sales were not held every day. In the market place a low stage would be erected so that those who were to be sold might be more readily displayed to public view. Gomer, showing all the signs of a vice-ridden life, was one of those to be auctioned that day. The slaves would stand on the platform naked so that potential buyers could see all the flaws. It was now time for Gomer to be auctioned and she was led forward to stand in front of the crowd. 'Who will give an omer for Gomer?' jokes the auctioneer. A ripple of laughter flits across the crowd. Gomer was not much of a prize. Her best days were long behind her. 'Come along now, there must be someone who wants her!' Then at the back of the crowd a hand goes up. 'Me! I will pay the price for her.' It is Hosea who pays the redemption price for his own wife. He clothes her and takes her home.

Isn't that what Christ has done for sinners? We have played the harlot and have had many lovers in the world, and we have paid the price for our rebellion. There is no longer anything about us that is desirable. We stand, as it were, naked for all our faults to be seen. Can God ever look upon me with delight? Can he look upon you and take pleasure in you? We stare down at our feet and confess we cannot see how it can be so.

There are many titles for Christ in Scripture. Some speak of his glory, of his excellence, of his power, or of his majesty. Among my favourite are those descriptions given in the Song of Solomon: He is 'the chiefest among ten thousand' (5:10 KJV), yea he is 'altogether lovely' (5:16 KJV). Even those words seem too mean to describe my lovely Master and noble Lord. But how they do cause the heart to leap with praise.

But if we are to take to heart the wondrous truth that *God is always better than we can imagine* there is yet more that we can say.

There is another description of Christ. It is a title that was given not by those who loved him. Such a title might be disparaged as biased by those who hated him and sought to destroy him. We have, therefore, no option but to assume that if both follower and detractor hold the statement to be accurate, then there is literally no argument. It was the enemies of Jesus who spoke of him as the 'friend of sinners' (Matt. 11;19; Luke 7:34). I can tell you this: I am no university professor; I am no great pillar of the church; for good reason I am not asked onto the platform of the well-known conferences. But I can tell you this: I am a sinner. Yes, that's me—a sinner. But, oh! how I love that title: 'Jesus, the Friend of Sinners.' That's where my confidence lies.

Now, dear reader, perhaps you look back upon your life and there is altogether too much of the Gomer about you. You find yourself in the midst of a 'famine,' and all around bespeaks the judgment of God. Have you grounds for despair? Not while God remains always better than you can imagine.

How does our text conclude? Here it is; read it again:

> They say, If a man put away his wife, and she go from him, and become another man's, shall he return unto her again? shall not that land be greatly polluted? but thou hast played the harlot with many lovers; yet return again to me, saith the LORD.

'*Yet return again to me.*' Whether you have remained in a backslidden state for months or years, or have never come to Christ at all, then hear the gracious invitation. He who is better than you can imagine says, 'Return again to me.'

For further reflection:

1. What would it take to bring a nation (back) to God?

2. What does God see in you?

3. Is there still hope for sinners in the God of grace?

Meditation 15

What Does an Omniscient God Not Remember?

'Behold, the days are coming,' declares the LORD, when I will make a new covenant with the house of Israel and the house of Judah, not like the covenant that I made with their fathers on the day when I took them by the hand to bring them out of the land of Egypt, my covenant that they broke, though I was their husband,' declares the LORD. 'But this is the covenant that I will make with the house of Israel after those days, declares the LORD: I will put my law within them, and I will write it on their hearts. And I will be their God, and they shall be my people. And no longer shall each one teach his neighbour and each his brother, saying, "Know the LORD," for they shall all know me, from the least of them to the greatest, declares the LORD. For I will forgive their iniquity, and I will remember their sin no more.'—Jeremiah 31:31-34.

The story starts off in an ordinary enough sort of way; 'In the spring of the year, the time when kings go out to battle, David sent Joab ...' But stop and think. Who is king? David is. Where should the king be? With his army. Where was he? In Jerusalem. The chronicler has said nothing explicitly to condemn the king, but in one sentence we are told he wasn't where he should have been, and we are now expecting trouble.

While his generals and soldiers were risking their lives in battle, David was taking the evening air. Looking down from the palace roof he saw Bathsheba bathing. There's no way to soften this. He was overcome with lust and sent for her. He slept with her and she became pregnant. To cover over his sin, he sent for her husband, Uriah the Hittite – he's not even an Israelite but yet he is fighting for David. Uriah was a more honourable man at this point than the king, and he refused to go home to his wife while his comrades-in-arms were roughing it at the battlefront. David tried again to get Uriah to spend a night at home with his wife but failed. He therefore sent Uriah back to his general Joab with a note in his hand which was effectively his death warrant. So not only does David commit adultery with Uriah's wife, he cunningly planned to have him killed and even got the unsuspecting man himself to carry the instructions. This was not David's finest hour.

For a time David thought he had got away with adultery and murder. Until that is Nathan, the prophet came to see the king. Nathan told David a story about a rich man with large flocks, and a poor man with just one little ewe lamb—more like a pet than a sheep. The rich man had taken the poor man's darling lamb to feed some recently arrived guests. David was incensed at the injustice of what he had heard. Then comes what must surely be one of the most dramatic moments in Scripture history; certainly one of the most dramatic lines: you can imagine Nathan fixing David with his eye and firmly saying in a loud clear voice, 'You are the man!'

Nathan words have pierced David through to David's calloused heart. The king who could take another man's wife and have her husband killed, is now crushed by the weight of his own sin. 'My sin is ever before me,' he laments.

Few men have done what David did. But then, few men have had the opportunity. Think about that the next time you are praying for promotion! Perhaps the reason the Lord graciously withholds it from you is that you would abuse the increased authority just the way David did. It may be the Lord's mercy to you that he withholds it!

The truth is that even if we have not committed all the sins in the catalogue, all too often we have allowed to grow in our hearts the root of one particular sin, even if the full mature fruit is not so obvious. Or, to put it another way, while we are congratulating ourselves that we have not plumbed the depths of sin, we are quite content to dip a toe into the water's edge. We think others foolish who have drowned themselves in the ocean, but we are paddling in the same ocean's shallows.

David recognized that his sin was more than a minor inconvenience. 'Against you only have I sinned, and done what is evil in your sight.' It's the work of the Holy Spirit to bring men under conviction. David was brought under a sense of conviction by the preaching of Nathan, just as many in the crowd were brought to feel the weight of their sin at Pentecost by Peter's preaching. Cut to the heart they cried out, 'What then shall we do?' To which Peter replied, 'Repent!'

Better by far to have God's forgiveness than all the riches of this world, for what will it profit a man if he should gain the whole world but lose his soul?

But will God forgive my sins? What encouragement does he give me? Much every way!

I love the way in which Hezekiah talks about God's dealing with his sins; 'You have cast all my sins behind your back' (Isa. 38:17). Now what is the picture here? God has taken Hezekiah's sins and put them where God can't see them. Of course, God doesn't have a 'back' behind which to put anything, but Hezekiah's confidence is that when the Lord removes them, it is as though he has placed them where they are no longer in view. The eye of the all-seeing God no longer looks upon them.

Here is how Micah encourages the saints:

> Who is a God like you, pardoning iniquity and passing over transgression for the remnant of his inheritance? He does not retain his anger forever, because he delights in steadfast love. He will

again have compassion on us; he will tread our iniquities under foot. You will cast all our sins into the depths of the sea (Mic. 7:19).

The picture is a clear one. Once you drop something into the depths of the sea, it is gone for good. There is no getting it back.

The most striking illustration of all comes from Jeremiah; 'I will forgive their iniquity, and I will remember their sin no more' (Jer. 31:34). Now just how is it possible for an omniscient (i.e. all-knowing) God to forget our sins? Actually that's not exactly what he promises. It would be strange indeed if God were to be forgetful.

But *God is always better than we can imagine.* We would have been content though unable to explain how God could forget our sins, but when he says he will remember them no more, he is actually telling us something infinitely better.

Let me illustrate. Suppose two friends have a disagreement and things are said by one to the other that ought not to be said. Later the friend who said too much goes to the other and confesses, 'What I said was wrong and I am asking you to forgive me.' Now the friend has a choice to make. Does he forgive his friend or not? If he is a Christian he is required to forgive when asked, but what is he doing when he says, 'I forgive'? He is saying that the matter is concluded, the friend has sought and received forgiveness, and the friend sinned against is making a promise not to bring it up again. If he does he hasn't really forgiven. That's what God is doing in forgiveness. In repentance we acknowledge our sin and ask God to forgive us. When he grants forgiveness he is making a promise that he will not bring our sin up again; He will remember it no more.

> My sin, oh, the bliss of this glorious thought!
> My sin, not in part but the whole,
> Is nailed to the cross, and I bear it no more;
> Praise the Lord, praise the Lord, O my soul!

The omniscient God is also the God of all grace, who takes my sin, places it where he cannot see it, casts it into the depths of the sea, and will remember it no more.

For further reflection:

1. What are the three descriptions of how God deals with your sin?

2. Do you sometimes think you have got away with sin?

3. How did Nathan stir David's conscience?

Meditation 16

When the Disaster Is the Blessing

Then Nebuchadnezzar in furious rage commanded that Shadrach, Meshach, and Abednego be brought. So they brought these men before the king. Nebuchadnezzar answered and said to them, 'Is it true, O Shadrach, Meshach, and Abed-nego, that you do not serve my gods or worship the golden image that I have set up? Now if you are ready when you hear the sound of the horn, pipe, lyre, trigon, harp, bagpipe, and every kind of music, to fall down and worship the image that I have made, well and good. But if you do not worship, you shall immediately be cast into a burning fiery furnace. And who is the god who will deliver you out of my hands?' Shadrach, Meshach, and Abed-nego answered and said to the king, 'O Nebuchadnezzar, we have no need to answer you in this matter. If this be so, our God whom we serve is able to deliver us from the burning fiery furnace, and he will deliver us out of your hand, O king. But if not, be it known to you, O king, that we will

> not serve your gods or worship the golden image
> that you have set up.' — Daniel 3:13-18.

I remember the first ordination that I attended after I was installed as a minister of a congregation. It was a rather formal affair. Not only did all the ministers of the Presbytery enter in solemn procession in pairs to fill the front pews but they did so in strict order of seniority, that is, with those most recently ordained, like me, at the front and the greybeards at the back. Each was sombrely attired in a black cassock and Geneva gown with the academic hood of the respective alma mater adding the only splash of colour.

I've found that ordination services on the other side of the Atlantic from my native Scotland are considerably less formal. After the Presbytery has met, the individual ministers and elders make their way into the church to sit wherever they want. The idea of a procession with which to begin the proceedings is really quite alien. So, I confess that there lingers a part of me that hankers after a little more formality to lend the event a greater sense of occasion. Would the bride be any less married if she were not in her bridal gown? Of course not. But most would feel disappointed if there were not something to mark the event as being special.

When it came to a sense of occasion few can compete with Nebuchadnezzar. On an appointed day he called together the satraps, the prefects, and the governors, the counsellors, the treasurers, the justices, the magistrates, and all the officials of the provinces. Each would have the insignia and robes of his particular office. No doubt they would have been brought forward and seated according to precedence (that's the way of royal courts). But what is the point of having such a splendid occasion without appropriate music? Nebuchadnezzar had thought of that too. He had arranged a large orchestra composed of horn, pipe, lyre, trigon, harp, bagpipe, and every kind of music to guide the proceedings. It makes sense. When you are marshalling a large crowd, it is so much easier if the 'commands' are given by way of the sound of a trumpet or, better still, an entire orchestra. There is a limit as to how far the human voice can travel with ease.

And the occasion for Nebuchadnezzar? He had set up on the plain of Dura, a gold statue, and all the members of government, senior and junior, were there to bow to it and worship it. How tempting it is for us to suppose that those present thought that Nebuchadnezzar had discovered a new god, and they were only too delighted to do the needful! If that were the case, we could sit back with a comfortable air of superiority smiling benignly on these rather naive and primitive people. But was that really what was going on?

The long list of participants was also an indication of a variety of different languages represented, and if there were different languages there would have been different cultures. Nebuchadnezzar was not king of a small parcel of land so much as the supreme ruler of a vast empire. The purpose of the day was not so much religious as political.

He made no demands on those assembled to leave the worship of whatever local deity was favoured, so long as they recognized the statue that he had set up. This was not so different to the emperors of Rome centuries later. The followers of Jesus were free to worship their Saviour, no matter how repellant the Romans thought him, so long as they would also worship the emperor—in other words, if they demonstrated their loyalty to Rome by doing so. For Shadrach, Meshach and Abed-nego, as for their spiritual descendants in the early centuries after the ascension of Jesus, and down to the present day, that was something they could not in conscience do.

In the large assembly, though, who would notice whether three men would bend the knee or not? Perhaps if everyone else had their foreheads touching the ground, they would stick out, but in such cases there are always those on hand to make sure that God's people get into trouble. There were those who made it their business to bring it to the attention of the king. The king was furious. It is not surprising. He was personally invested in the event. It wasn't just that considerable resources had been put into a statue approximately 90 feet tall, made or at least covered in gold, or that Nebuchadnezzar had hired the Babylon Philharmonic Orchestra for the day (and they don't come cheap!), it was the challenge to his authority that threw him into a rage.

The whole event was staged to bring cohesion to a vast and somewhat unwieldy empire. This was to give focus and a degree of stability to a diverse political structure of different nations, tongues and peoples. And Shadrach, Meshach and Abednego were ruining it all.

Compliance was all Nebuchadnezzar desired. He even gave them a second chance. Better to have compliance with some excuse that they did not understand the instructions than to make their defiance obvious by killing them on the spot. But so that there should be no misunderstanding, let it be clear that when they heard the Babylon Philharmonic strike up again, Shadrach and his friends had better be there with the rest of the worshippers with their foreheads touching the ground.

It can take courage to face down an angry man under the best of circumstances. How much more when the man is a potentate with power of life and death who feels that his own dignity has been challenged. Yet the response was simple. 'We don't need to answer you on this matter.' The King James Version (KJV) says they don't have to be careful. In other words they are not looking for a diplomatic solution to get them out of a tricky situation. On the contrary, the God whom they worship, can save and will save, but even if he does not—or at least does not appear to save them, Shadrach, Meshach and Abednego will not bend the knee.

Nebuchadnezzar ordered that the furnace be heated seven times hotter than its usual temperature, probably to match the heat of his own anger. The heat was so intense that the elite troops who were commissioned with the task of tossing the troublesome rebels into the fire were themselves consumed.

Meanwhile Shadrach, Meshach and Abed-nego were joined in the fiery furnace by one that, in the eyes of Nebuchadnezzar, looked like a son of one of the gods.

There are a number of lessons to be drawn from this wonderful story of three men who loved God more than their own lives. The most obvious may be that there are times when we will face persecution for no other reason than being faithful to the Lord. Hardship is not necessarily a sign of God's disfavour. Remember the disciples in the boat on the see of Galilee? Jesus had dismissed the crowd to their homes and ordered, not *suggested* or *agreed* to the disciples getting into the boat. The storm arose and their lives were in peril because they were obedient to the commandment of their master. In Matthew's account we are told the boat was being *tortured* by the wind and waves.

We might draw comfort from the fact that Shadrach, Meshach and Abednego were ultimately rescued from the fiery furnace, though their own willingness to recognize that sometimes God does not rescue us in the way we expect or desire should be a caution to us.

In the midst of the storm it is natural for us to wish that the winds and waves would cease. We would even be quite willing to give God the glory for his sovereign stilling of the tempest if we might once more regain a tranquil life. But sometimes God shows his might not by stilling the powerful storm but by taking the frail boat and steering it through the roughest seas to a safe haven. Speaking personally, I've been in a Force 10 gale at sea, and I much prefer smooth sailing. It takes the courage of Shadrach, Meshach and Abed-nego to say, whatever happens we will trust in our God.

But in keeping with the theme of this slim volume, we can see that *God is always better than we can imagine.* The alternatives that suggest themselves to us are, the stilling of the storm or that the Lord would let the storm continue and show his power and glory by taking us through the wind and waves.

But I think we can see a third possibility emerging from the story of the three godly men of Daniel 3. Imagine for a moment that you have the opportunity to go back and speak to one of those brave fellow believers as he is about to be taken home to glory. As you reflect with him on his past life and the Lord's gracious dealings with him, you ask, 'What is the event that sticks out most prominently in your mind.' I don't think we do violence to Scripture to say that his answer would be, 'The fiery furnace.' 'And what was it about the fiery furnace that was most memorable?' 'Ah,' he says, 'It was when "one like a son of the gods" walked with us in the midst of the fire.'

So which is better? Not to have trials but be without Christ, or to have trials—even fiery trials (1 Pet. 4:12)— but to have Christ with us? Timid hearts shy away from the trials, but sometimes the trials are indeed the blessing.

For further reflection:

1. Why do you think Nebuchadnezzar set up the statue to be worshipped?

2. What was more important to Shadrach, Meshach and Abed-nego than obeying the king?

3. Did the three young men make the right choice?

Meditation 17

Peter's Boast

Now when Jesus came into the district of Caesarea Philippi, he asked his disciples, 'Who do
people say that the Son of Man is?' And they said,
'Some say John the Baptist, others say Elijah, and
others Jeremiah or one of the prophets.' He said
to them, 'But who do you say that I am?' Simon
Peter replied, 'You are the Christ, the Son of the
living God.' And Jesus answered him, 'Blessed
are you, Simon Bar-Jonah! For flesh and blood
has not revealed this to you, but my Father who
is in heaven. And I tell you, you are Peter, and on
this rock I will build my church, and the gates
of hell shall not prevail against it. I will give you
the keys of the kingdom of heaven, and whatever
you bind on earth shall be bound in heaven, and
whatever you loose on earth shall be loosed in
heaven.' Then he strictly charged the disciples to
tell no one that he was the Christ. From that time
Jesus began to show his disciples that he must
go to Jerusalem and suffer many things from the

elders and chief priests and scribes, and be killed, and on the third day be raised. And Peter took him aside and began to rebuke him, saying, 'Far be it from you, Lord! This shall never happen to you.' But he turned and said to Peter, 'Get behind me, Satan! You are a hindrance to me. For you are not setting your mind on the things of God, but on the things of man.' Then Jesus told his disciples, 'If anyone would come after me, let him deny himself and take up his cross and follow me. For whoever would save his life will lose it, but whoever loses his life for my sake will find it. For what will it profit a man if he gains the whole world and forfeits his life? Or what shall a man give in return for his life? For the Son of Man is going to come with his angels in the glory of his Father, and then he will repay each person according to what he has done. Truly, I say to you, there are some standing here who will not taste death until they see the Son of Man coming in his kingdom.' — Matthew 16:13-23.

Peter had a gift, though perhaps 'gift' isn't quite the right word. He could put two words into a sentence that really don't belong together. The two words are 'No' and 'Lord.'

Take for example the time when Jesus asked his disciples what people were saying about him. You can imagine the conversation. 'I heard someone say he thought you were John the Baptist come back from the dead.' 'Yes, and someone else said he thought you were possibly Elijah.'

Then a third chips in, 'Sure, most people seem to think you are one of the prophets.'

But then Jesus turns the conversation to them. 'What about you, then? Who do you say that I am?'

You have probably noticed that Peter is often the spokesman for the group. In fact he had a tendency to engage his mouth before putting his brain in gear, hence his special 'gift,' but we love him all the more for it. On this occasion Peter is the first to declare to Jesus, 'You are the Christ!' ('Christ' is the Greek word for 'Messiah' or the Anointed One.)

That was a really momentous declaration. The people of God had been waiting for the Messiah since God made the promise to Adam and Eve before evicting them from the Garden of Eden, and Peter had just declared that here he was standing right in front of them: 'You are the Messiah!'

After thousands of years of waiting, certain expectations had arisen, not all of which were true to the Bible's teaching. In fact many expectations with respect to the Messiah had nothing to do with what God had promised at all. This is the reason why Jesus immediately began to tell them what his disciples ought to expect. The Messiah had to suffer many things. He would not be welcomed by the elders. Rather he would be rejected by them and by the chief priests and the teachers of the law, and worse still, he would be killed; but after three days he would rise again.

Now though common folk saw something special in Jesus, they had not confessed him to be the Messiah. It was the disciples who had seen that truth. But they too had their own ideas of the work the Messiah would do. You can almost see Peter taking Jesus by the sleeve, and quietly speaking into his ear: 'Excuse me, Jesus, but do you mind if I have a quiet word with you about what you have to do as Messiah? I think you've really got the wrong idea, and I need to put you right on a few things.'

Whether Peter had intended it to be a quiet word or not, Jesus made it public. This was too important a matter to be misunderstood. Peter didn't have in mind the things of God but the things of men. What a short step it was from 'Blessed are you, Peter!' to 'Get behind me, Satan!'

Many years later, Peter was in Caesarea. One day he went up on the roof terrace to pray while the food was being prepared for the midday meal. As he prayed God gave him a vision of what looked like a large sheet being let down from heaven by its corners. In the sheet were all kinds of 'unclean' animals, which according to the Jewish dietary laws, were forbidden to be eaten. Well, it was lunchtime and Peter was hungry. The voice he heard in the vision told him to 'Kill and eat!'

'Surely not, Lord!' was Peter's response. Oh, Peter, not again! There it is, 'No, Lord!'

Perhaps Peter was thinking of Ezekiel who was told to do something that would make him unclean, and of how God modified the plan.

There is another occasion recorded in the Bible when we find Peter wanting to rewrite the Lord's plans. It happened just before Jesus was arrested. The Lord warned the disciples of what was about to happen. Here is the account as given in the Gospels of Matthew and Luke which I have placed together:

> Jesus said, 'Simon, Simon, behold, Satan demanded to have you, that he might sift you like wheat, but I have prayed for you that your faith may not fail. And when you have turned again, strengthen your brothers.'
>
> Peter said to him, 'Lord, I am ready to go with you both to prison and to death.' He also said to Jesus 'Though they all fall away because of you, I will never fall away.'
>
> Jesus said to him, 'Truly, I tell you, this very night, before the rooster crows, you will deny me three times.'
>
> Peter said to him, 'Even if I must die with you, I will not deny you!'

So, here we have it again. Bold Peter ready to go to prison and to death. But did he? Those who know their Bibles well know that he did not. Actually, it didn't take much to cause him to crumble. Just a servant girl's innocent question. She wasn't much of a threat really. It wasn't as if Peter was pinned to the wall, with a sword at his throat, by some Roman soldier eager to spill his blood on a Jerusalem street. No, it was just a servant girl, and then, moments later, a passerby who thought his Galilean accent gave him away as a follower of Jesus.

Peter trumpeted his love for Jesus: he was ready to die for his Lord. But, of course, and according to God's plan, it was Jesus who died for Peter. I wonder how many times afterwards did Peter remember Jesus' words on the night of his arrest: 'Greater love hath no man than this that a man lay down his life for his friends,' especially the very next sentence which is surely deliberate, 'You are my friends …'

Jesus himself sets the measure of love; a love so great that one is willing to lay down one's life for a friend. Indeed we can scarcely envisage the circumstances under which such a sacrifice *could* be made; harder still to envisage the circumstances under which it *would* be made.

It is as much as we can do to stretch our imaginations. Perhaps we could imagine a child of ours lying gravely ill in hospital; would we not be willing to have an organ removed to save a life?

But think on this: God is always better than we can imagine. 'But God shows his love for us in that *while we were still sinners*, Christ died for us' (Rom. 5:8). Or, again, 'For if *while we were enemies* we were reconciled to God by the death of his Son, how much more, now that we are reconciled, shall we be saved by his life' (Rom. 5:10). Do you see? It was not because we were friends with God that he sent his Son to die for us. It was because he died for us that we are his friends. Never was there love like this.

> Were the whole realm of nature mine,
>   That were an offering far too small;
> Love so amazing, so divine,
>   Demands my soul, my life, my all.

For further reflection:

1. What about you, who do you say that Jesus is?

2. Do you boast of what you will do for Jesus or of what he has done for you?

3. Did Christ die for his friends or his enemies and what does it tell us of his love?

Meditation 18

Remuneration Instead of Recrimination

> Now after a long time the master of those serv-
> ants came and settled accounts with them. And
> he who had received the five talents came for-
> ward, bringing five talents more, saying, 'Master,
> you delivered to me five talents; here I have made
> five talents more.' His master said to him, 'Well
> done, good and faithful servant. You have been
> faithful over a little; I will set you over much.
> Enter into the joy of your master.' And he also
> who had the two talents came forward, saying,
> 'Master, you delivered to me two talents; here I
> have made two talents more.' His master said to
> him, 'Well done, good and faithful servant. You
> have been faithful over a little; I will set you over
> much. Enter into the joy of your master.'
>
> —Matthew 25:19-23.

Spurgeon told a story about a soldier in Napoleon's army.
Whatever was his offence the penalty was death. The sol-
dier's mother approached Napoleon to plead for mercy.
The French Emperor asked the distraught mother why

the soldier deserved mercy. The answer of the mother was disarmingly simple: if he deserved anything it wouldn't be mercy.

I sometimes wonder if a consequence of the Covenant of Works is that we are all hard-wired in favour of justification by works. I have never encountered the unbeliever who does not think that in some way he deserves God's favour. He may be quite willing to concede that there are certain individuals who for their terrible crimes against humanity deserve hell: people like Stalin and Hitler. But ordinary folks—the sort we meet each day—are not contemplating mass extermination and want only to be left in peace, and to leave others to get on with their own lives. If there is a hell, there are going to be remarkably few people there—or at least so the theory goes.

If you are able to find the right occasion to speak to someone about the needs of his soul and he is willing to discuss the matter, with only rare exception will you find anyone who does not believe that the pearly gates will inevitably open to them when they knock for admittance. After all, you really have to work hard to have the gates shut in your face. In fact, the occurrence of someone who believes there is a God but is not trusting in Christ, thinking that he is going to a lost eternity, is so rare, that I have yet to encounter him. I put the suggestion forward as a logical possibility, but there may not be anyone in that class.

It is an opinion which is confirmed just about every time you go to a an unbeliever's funeral, even that of a rank unbeliever. I went to the funeral of a doctor who was well known for his antagonism to the church and for his antipathy for the things of God. The preacher who took the service seemed to be preaching 'justification by death.' What do you have to do to get into heaven? Simply die! Mocking God apparently would not keep you out.

I say we are hard-wired for works righteousness because, as I know my own heart, I know how swiftly we can fall back into such a way of thinking. Just check your own thoughts for a moment. Have you ever found yourself in a moment of great trial trying to strike up a bargain with God? 'Lord, if you will heal my child, I will …' Fill in the missing words yourself. Of course any parent will sacrifice much for a beloved child. I have heard of couples who have sold their home to pay the medical bills, or who have handed over their retirement savings to pay a lawyer's bill to keep a son out of prison.

It is because it comes so naturally to us that we need to be all the more vigilant to guard our souls against it, especially when the text seems to be nudging us in that direction. Take the parable of the three servants who received five, two and one talent respectively. The one who had been given five talents doubled the sum, as did the one who had received two. The servant who received the one talent hid it in the ground and gave it back to his master on his return. The servant who presented his master with the original five talents plus the five he had made from business, was put in charge of many things. Likewise the servant who had doubled the two talents he had received.

The servant who had been given the single talent but who had not invested it at all, had it taken from him, and it was given to the one who had five. Well, that does rather sound like earning yourself a reward. But let's think more closely about what he has been said and done. Whose were the talents to begin with? They were, of course, the master's. He chose to give the talents to whom he desired to give them. Was the master under any obligation to give his servants any talents at all? The answer must be, No! Did the talents remain the property of the master? Yes. Could he have returned at any time and required that they be returned? Yes. Were they at all times the master's for him to dispose of according to his pleasure?

Now consider the responsibility of the three servants. I have called them *servants* but the text actually refers to them as *slaves*. I called them servants because I did not wish to cloud the parable with the rights and wrongs of slavery! But the designation cannot be avoided any longer. The three men who were entrusted with the talents were slaves, that is they were the property of their master. As such the understanding of the time would be that not only were the talents the property of the master to do with as he saw fit, but also the men themselves. It was their obligation to serve their master; to be 'well pleasing' as Paul wrote to Titus. To put it another way, it was the slaves' responsibility to do the best they could with the talents entrusted to their care.

Jesus spoke of the slave who had been out all day in the field ploughing and then coming into the master's house.

Would the master tell the slave to sit down while he, the master, prepared the meal for his slave? That would be ludicrous. The slave should remove the dirt from under his nails and dress properly before serving the master his dinner. So, what is the point? The point is that the slaves in both stories only did what they were supposed to do. They had not earned their reward. It was given to them from grace.

A proper understanding of the role and responsibilities of the three slaves leads into what Jesus has to say next.

What about the end—the end of everything? Everyone will be there? Not metaphorically but literally! You will be there, as will I. Then will take place the great division. Scripture only ever speaks of sheep and goats, wheat and tares, those who belong to Christ and those who do not. Jesus presents a picture of the assembling together of all humanity. First he will speak to the sheep: those who trust in him. They receive the blessing prepared for them. But he also gives an explanation. The shepherd says he was fed by the sheep, watered by them, welcomed by them, clothed by them, cared for and visited by them. This leaves the sheep bewildered. There is a sort of collective befuddlement. 'When did we do that? I don't remember doing that for you.'

The picture moves from a shepherd separating out the sheep and the goats to the king making an authoritative statement. 'When you did it for one of mine, even the least, you did it to me!' Perhaps familiarity or lack of concentrated thought robs us sometimes of the sheer magnificence of a text. What is Jesus saying here? His eye is so acute that when a seemingly insignificant event such as someone giving a glass of water to one of Christ's less notable followers, he sees it and takes note of it. We forget that we have done it. It escapes our recollection. But not one is forgotten by the Lord. It is treasured up by him.

The goats by contrast will be condemned for failing to feed, water, clothe, etc. the Lord's people. They too will make much the same response but from the other side. 'When did we see you hungry and not feed you?' Does that mean that they lived utterly selfish lives and never gave a glass of water to a thirsty child? No, it is not saying that; but it is saying that they were not motivated by love for Christ. Of course wealthy people should use their wealth wisely but it doesn't matter how many hospitals or schools a wealthy man endows if he does not do it for Christ.

But our great and noble theme is to see how great God is, and to stretch our minds to see still more. It is in the response first of the master then of the Shepherd King that we begin to see something of his beauty, tenderness and grace. It is not being placed in charge of many things that arrests the attention, it is the simple welcome, so beautifully captured in the KJV: 'Enter thou into the joy of thy Lord.' Now if we see beyond the simple story to what Jesus is saying, we will be lifted up in adoration. You don't deserve anything from God except his condemnation. Neither do I. But we wretched rebels are bid enter into the joy of our Lord. Why should God take pleasure in you and me? I have no idea. I can't tell you how he could take pleasure in me. All I can tell you is this: that having the benediction of God is better than the crowns and governments of all the kingdoms of the earth!

But there is more. *God is always better than we can imagine.*

Jesus goes on to tell us that the blessing he has in store for us has been prepared from the foundation of the world. From the beginning he has been preparing a blessing. That tells us something by itself. King George VI died in 1952, but Elizabeth II was not crowned until 1953. Why? Simply because it took that long to organize the event. The more significant the event the longer it takes to plan. Few are those who get engaged and married in the same week!

But there is something more still. Jesus announces what we will receive. We are to inherit the kingdom. He has prepared the kingdom for us. Now stop to compare that with the expectations of your average unbeliever. He thinks he will have earned some sort of reward by his good deeds. The believer can only reply, 'Dear friend, you really don't know God. You think you deserve something and your expectation is based on yourself. I don't deserve anything but my expectation is based on God!' Grace will give us infinitely more than what we think we might achieve for ourselves, because God is always better than we can imagine.

It is amazing! Stupefying! Glorious! Best by far, however, is simply to hear those words from Jesus himself:

'Come, ye blessed of my Father!' The benediction alone is worth more than this world can offer.

For further reflection:

1. What is the misplaced level of expectation of reward for the unbeliever?

2. What is the promise of reward given to the believer?

3. What does this world have to compare with what God promises you?

Meditation 19

The Blessing in What Jesus Did Not Say

> And he came to Nazareth, where he had been brought up. And as was his custom, he went to the synagogue on the Sabbath day, and he stood up to read. And the scroll of the prophet Isaiah was given to him. He unrolled the scroll and found the place where it was written, 'The Spirit of the Lord is upon me, because he has anointed me to proclaim good news to the poor. He has sent me to proclaim liberty to the captives and recovering of sight to the blind, to set at liberty those who are oppressed, to proclaim the year of the Lord's favor.' And he rolled up the scroll and gave it back to the attendant and sat down. And the eyes of all in the synagogue were fixed on him. —Luke 4:16-20.

What do you do to pass the time on a long car journey? One 'game' I have used with my own family and with young people on a mission trip is to ask them, if they could be any person from the Bible, who would they choose to be and why. Try it with your own family.

I'll give you my Bible character. It is John the beloved disciple. Just his very description as 'the disciple whom Jesus loved' is enough. But I have other reasons. As the disciples reclined at table at the last supper, John was next to Jesus. He was so close that all he had to do was lean back and he would be resting his head on Jesus. Oh, to be so close to Jesus that a slight movement would find me wholly leaning on him!

So what Christian has not at some point wondered what it must have been like to be alive in Israel when Jesus was walking the earth? Surely it must have been exciting to have seen him feed the five thousand, or cure lepers, or make the blind see, the deaf hear, the lame walk. What about being with Jesus when he called Lazarus out of the tomb? I think I would have been like the Queen of Sheba whose breath was taken away when she saw for herself the glory, the magnificence, and the splendour of Solomon's royal court.

Not so dramatic but no less important, I would have loved to hear Jesus speak of the things of God. He spoke with authority and not as the scribes. There must have been something about his conversation that was really quite different to that of other men. You can get a sense of it from the disciples. On one occasion Jesus is praying, but we can be assured of this: when Jesus communed with his Father in heaven, it lifted prayer on to an altogether higher plain. No wonder the disciples' immediate response is 'Lord, teach us how to pray!' They were as much as saying, 'Whatever we have been doing up until now, isn't *real* prayer, now that we have heard you! Teach us how to have such fellowship with our heavenly Father!' It may not have been as dramatic as hearing Jesus declare, 'Lazarus, come forth!' but it was soul-stirring nonetheless.

Today as we continue our meditations on God and how he is always better than we can imagine, I want to take us to the synagogue in Nazareth so that we might sit at the feet of Jesus. We are not going to be contemplating Jesus walking on water or stilling a storm. We shall not be thinking of him driving out demons or healing a man with a withered hand. Instead we are going to observe him opening up the Scriptures. And really that is more important by far.

On this occasion Jesus was coming home. Nazareth was the town in which he was raised. He had spent his entire life until that point working as a carpenter. To begin with he learned the trade from Joseph but perhaps after Joseph's death he took responsibility for the family business and provided for his widowed mother Mary. How many of those in the synagogue that day had at one time or another brought their plough or table or chair to Jesus to have it repaired? He had done a good job as a carpenter; and now he appeared to have developed a better than average grasp of Scripture. Clearly he had studied hard to master the Torah. He seemed to have insights into the sacred writings that others just did not have. And now here he was back among his own people. It was natural to pass the scroll to him for him to read and deliver a homily. The elder of the synagogue handed the scroll of

Isaiah to Jesus for on that Sabbath the reading was to be taken from that prophet. He unrolled the scroll until he came to the portion we know as chapter 61, which was almost at the end of the scroll. With a clear voice he read the words carefully:

> The Spirit of the Lord GOD is upon me,
> because the LORD has anointed me to bring good
>   news to the poor;
>   he has sent me to bind up the brokenhearted,
> to proclaim liberty to the captives,
> and the opening of the prison to those who are
>   bound;
>   to proclaim the year of the LORD's favor.

It's not a long reading. Actually, it is only one verse and a little into the next. As readings go, it is pretty short.

After he had read from the scroll, he rolled it up again and handed it back to the attendant and sat down, as was the custom, to teach. The eyes of everyone in the synagogue were fastened on him. They could not possibly have anticipated what he was going to say to them next. 'Today this Scripture is fulfilled in your hearing.'

Now to claim that any Old Testament prophecy was being fulfilled in the presence of his hearers would have been staggering. But this particular one! As he continued to speak everyone was amazed at the gracious words that came from his lips. God's Spirit had anointed Jesus and he came with a message—and O what a message! Each line resonated with the grace and goodness of God. Even as a preacher (perhaps because I am a preacher), I hesitate to expound the text. How can my stumbling words compare with the gracious words of Jesus as he expounded the word of God in the synagogue of Nazareth that day. But even with the colossal weakness freely admitted, the message is one that brings hope to whosoever will receive it.

Jesus has come to bring 'good news'—the very origin of the word *gospel*. That gospel promised long before is good news for the poor. The kingdom of heaven is not the sole preserve of those who have the financial resources to secure it (as the rich young ruler was to discover). Those who have nothing can come, and buy and eat, without money and without price. There is good news for those who have struggled with sin and felt their condition to be beyond hope: Jesus came to proclaim freedom for such prisoners. There is good news for those who have taken up the Bible but who have found its meaning to be difficult and obscure. It was not only the eyes of the physically blind Jesus came to open. He also opens the eyes of those who are spiritually blind so that they may see. And for those who are oppressed there is good news too—the promise of release.

Jesus had come to proclaim the year of the Lord's favour. This idea is rooted in the year of jubilee in the Old Testament law. If a man fell into debt and had to sell himself into slavery to pay it off, then he could look to the future. At the end of every forty-nine years, a year of jubilee would be proclaimed, and those who had been enslaved would be released from their servitude. There was always hope. Do you see that? We can fall into debt through our own mismanagement or because of greed and other reasons; but though we have to bear the consequences for a season—perhaps a long season—God had provided a year of favour, a year of jubilee, a hope of release.

Now Jesus was in their midst to declare that the year of God's favour had arrived. It was good news for all who knew themselves in need of being set free.

You might think that this is as good as it gets.

> Long my imprisoned spirit lay
> Fast bound in sin and nature's night

as Charles Wesley wrote in a well known hymn. But there is a verse in that hymn which is not commonly sung:

> Still the small inward voice I hear,
> That whispers all my sins forgiven;
> Still the atoning blood is near,
> That quenched the wrath of hostile Heaven.
> I feel the life His wounds impart;
> I feel the Saviour in my heart.

Good news indeed for sinners! But there is more. *God is always better than we can imagine.*

Take a peek with me at the scroll from which Jesus read, and read a little further on. Here are the first two verse of Isaiah 61 in their entirety.

> The Spirit of the Lord GOD is upon me, because
> the LORD has anointed me to bring good news

to the poor; he has sent me to bind up the brokenhearted, to proclaim liberty to the captives, and the opening of the prison to those who are bound; to proclaim the year of the LORD's favour, and the day of vengeance of our God; to comfort all who mourn …

Do you see where Jesus stopped? Mid verse, mid sentence! It is as though Jesus would have nothing distract us from grace, wonderful grace!

This is good news! The God whom we worship is the 'God of all grace.' Tell your children. Tell your neighbours. Tell anyone who will listen to you. Today is the day of God's favour.

For further reflection:

1. What is the good news that Jesus proclaimed?

2. Is it good news for you?

3. Is it good news for your neighbour?

Meditation 20

Hired Hand or Son?

But when he came to himself, he said, 'How many of my father's hired servants have more than enough bread, but I perish here with hunger! I will arise and go to my father, and I will say to him, "Father, I have sinned against heaven and before you. I am no longer worthy to be called your son. Treat me as one of your hired servants."' And he arose and came to his father. But while he was still a long way off, his father saw him and felt compassion, and ran and embraced him and kissed him. And the son said to him, 'Father, I have sinned against heaven and before you. I am no longer worthy to be called your son.' But the father said to his servants, 'Bring quickly the best robe, and put it on him, and put a ring on his hand, and shoes on his feet. And bring the fattened calf and kill it, and let us eat and celebrate. For this my son was dead, and is alive again; he was lost, and is found.' And they began to celebrate.—Luke 15:17-24.

I think my favourite parable may be the parable of the Prodigal Son. I hope that as I explain why, you will understand my choice and perhaps make it your own favourite too.

At the beginning we are introduced to a man who had two sons. (Professor Finlayson, whom we will meet again in the next meditation, thought there were three sons, but that will have to wait.)

As the younger of two sons I was disappointed to find that the scoundrel in this family was the younger of the two. He was so ungrateful to and hateful of his father that he went up to him and said in not so many words, 'I can't wait for you to be dead so that I can get my hands on your money. Give it to me now!' As soon as he could liquidate the assets into cash he was off, and when I say he was off, he got as far away as he could. He evidently didn't want anything to do with his father and perhaps didn't want anything that would remind him of his father either.

In the 'far country' he began squandering his fortune by loose living, or as we might say, he threw his money away on fast cars and faster women. Perhaps we should stop at this point if we are going to understand the impact of the parable's ending. The younger son had taken all he could get from his father and used it for precisely what he wanted without a thought of the person to whom he owed everything. Now bear in mind that it is Jesus who is talking about the lost, and you will come to the conclusion that the Lord is describing the unconverted person's attitude towards God. It reminds me of a dinner conversation of which I heard many years ago. The philosopher C. E. M. Joad, who in his own day was as well known as George Bernard Shaw was, once asked what he thought of God. His reply was direct: 'I am more concerned to know what God thinks of me.' It's in this parable that Jesus answers that question—What does man look like from the vantage point of heaven?

Our unconverted friends and neighbours would be shocked to think that God has anything against them at all, let alone that they might be considered as the younger son is in this parable. But that is precisely what Jesus is saying. It is as though we have entered into God's presence and asked for all that we can get; all that we think we are entitled to. We take everything that God has to offer—our health, our strength, our abilities, our skills and whatever else might be on offer—and then we want nothing more to do with God at all. We don't even want to be reminded of him. For some, perhaps most, the very idea that we owe God anything at all is offensive. The attitude is that 'I have worked for everything I have!' Of course, if that is the controlling thought then God should be really very grateful for whatever we decide to give him, whether our time, treasure or talents. I am certainly not indebted to God for anything. The concept of worshiping God as the giver of all good gifts is utterly alien. But in truth every unbeliever has taken the gifts of God and has, or is now, squandering them on the things of this world without a thought for the Giver.

As with the prodigal so with the world—for a time we can live without God, but not for ever. In fact, as the story proceeds the best thing that could have happened to the prodigal son was to be put through a period of great need. If he had continued to have the resources to indulge his every fancy he never would have thought of returning to his father. It is a hard lesson to learn but sometimes the things we take the greatest delight in and would call 'blessings,' if we may use such a term, are actually the very things that hinder us from doing what we ought to do. Contrariwise, what we tend to think of as the greatest disasters may actually turn out to be the greatest blessings! That proved to be the case for the prodigal son.

He thought that having the resources to do exactly *what* he wanted and *when* he wanted was the best thing in the world. The blessing came in the form of a famine in the land. How clearly the Scriptures spell out the hardness of men's hearts. There was a severe famine in the land and the young man began to be in want. In other words, he was not driven back to his father by the first difficulty—the loss of his money. He tried to meet his problems out of his own resources. He attached himself to a local citizen who owned a herd of swine that needed someone to look after them. Now remember that Jesus is speaking to Jews. In fact at the beginning of the chapter we are told that this parable was spoken directly to the Pharisees and scribes. They would have got the point that the young man was doing something that was not just menial but actually detestable to any conscientious Jew. Then to drive the point home Jesus adds that the young man would have filled his stomach with pigswill if his stomach could have handled it. Presumably the pigswill wasn't kosher either.

How low can a man go? Low enough to envy unclean animals the garbage they are eating. It is a way of saying that he was at the end of all his resources. No man gave to him. We might add, and no man *could* give to him. What can this world give to a man who has had everything that this world can give? Only more of the same!

But then he came to himself! It was as though he had been in a coma and at last the reality of his situation was breaking in on him. What a fool he had been! His father had enough and to spare. His servants were well fed and well looked after and here he was living among the swine, wondering if there was anything in their food that he might be able to eat.

It was the famine in the land that had opened his eyes. What a blessing! Dear reader, could it be that you have taken the gifts of God but have only casually, erratically acknowledged the existence of your great benefactor; and the disaster that God has brought into your life is designed by him to bring you to your senses. Is that not evidence of the goodness of God? You might think that there are easier ways to get your attention, but all the things you count as blessings did not awaken you to your need. Perhaps there is someone somewhere praying right now that God would bring a famine into the land to bring you down to rock bottom low so that he will lift you up by his grace.

So, the younger son, now that he has come to his senses, realizes that being under his father's roof was actually better than anything this world has to offer. He makes up a little speech in his mind and rehearses what he is going to say when he sees the father whom he has so insulted and spurned: 'Father, I have sinned against heaven and in your sight. I am no longer worthy to be called your son; make me as one of your hired men.'

Even his request is instructive. The prodigal son does not ask to be a slave. Why not? Well, a slave is a member of the household and the owner, having invested in him, would wish to maintain his 'property.' It is the same with us and a car. The car I own I get serviced regularly because I maintain it and want to be still using it for years to come. Occasionally, I hire a car for a day or a weekend or even longer. When I do, I feel no obligation to take it in to have it serviced. When I have used it for the day, I hand it back. If it needs some maintenance that is someone else's responsibility.

So what was the son saying? 'Father, I have done you a great wrong. I am not fit to be your son. In fact I am not fit even to be a member of your household, but if you take me on as a daily labourer that's as much as I can ask. When I stop working at the end of the day and you pay me a day's wage, your obligation to me ceases.' What a come-down from being the heir of a very wealthy land-owner.

The hope of the son was to gain a few crusts so that he might not perish. But *God is always much better than we can imagine*, so although that was the thought of the young man, Jesus now turns the focus of the parable away from the young man to the father. One of my favourite lines in the Bible comes next. 'While he was still a long way off!' I can picture the father scanning the horizon day after day in the hope that his son would return. One day he is peering into the distance as he has done so many times before. It is too far to make out the features but there is something in his step that is unmistakable. It is his son! With no thought of decorum and taking no thought for the ingratitude and selfishness his son had shown him, he runs out to meet him. 'While he was *still* a long way off …' 'Still!' There was not a moment to lose. Right away! His heart was filled with love, and he went rushing towards the young man.

Now remember that this is a parable which Jesus told to Pharisees regarding tax collectors and sinners. The parable tells us of the love of the Father for the lost. It assures the sinner that when he comes to himself and returns to the Father in repentance, the Father (to use the vivid terms used in the parable) will rush out to meet him. How far away was he? Perhaps our theology will fill in what is missed out in the story. When the young man comes to himself and turns towards home, the shadow of his first footstep has not yet hit the ground when the Father rushes out to meet him.

The speech, well rehearsed as it is in the mind, was poured out before his father. The father hardly seems to notice, but embraces him, calls his slaves to bring the best robe, the ring, the sandals, and to kill the fatted calf and for the celebrations to begin. The joy of the father was unceasing and exuberant. The reason? 'This my son was lost and is found. He was dead and is alive again.'

There is another aspect which is not so obvious but is in the story nonetheless. Anyone who has ever lived near a pig farm knows that they smell. Locals might get used to it but visitors fear that the smell might leave a stain on their clothing—it is that bad. The prodigal son had no money to change his clothes. When he approached his father he would still have had the stench of the pigsty about him. But that does not stop the father from embracing him. Think of that the next time you think you have to clean yourself up before you come to God to ask for forgiveness—that's the devil's lie to stop you from coming.

So that there should be no mistake, Jesus tells us that there is joy in the presence of the angels in heaven over one sinner that repents.

Too often we end the telling of the story at that point. To do so is to miss the reason Jesus told this parable, as well as the two parables preceding it in Luke chapter 15.

Of course, the older brother was not too happy at the response of the father and felt that he had been treated unfairly. He was far from glad to hear that his brother was home, and he was more than a little annoyed that he was being fêted like a returning war hero. The younger went out and came back. The older went out and refused to come in. Perhaps in dealing with sinners we who have been around the Father's house a long time don't rejoice as we should—to our shame. If the angels in heaven rejoice, then surely we must too!

But there is more. Remember that third son of whom my old professor spoke—Professor Finlayson. He once told me that he thought there was another son and it is the third son that once more demonstrates that God is always better than we can imagine. 'You know,' he said, 'there was a third son, who saw the rebellion of the younger son and the hardness of the older brother.' Then with a smile he said, 'It is the Son who has come to show us the love the Father has for the lost and for those whose hearts do not rejoice in their salvation.' We would not know of the joy of heaven had not the Son come to tell us. Truly God is always better than we can imagine.

For further reflection:

1. With which of the sons in the parable do you identify?

2. What 'disasters' have you experienced that have turned out to be blessings?

3. How willing is God the Father to embrace you?

Meditation 21

The Thief Asked To Be Remembered and Was Promised Paradise

And one of the malefactors which were hanged railed on him, saying, If thou be Christ, save thyself and us. But the other answering rebuked him, saying, Dost not thou fear God, seeing thou art in the same condemnation? And we indeed justly; for we receive the due reward of our deeds: but this man hath done nothing amiss. And he said unto Jesus, Lord, remember me when thou comest into thy kingdom. And Jesus said unto him, Verily I say unto thee, To day shalt thou be with me in paradise. —Luke 23:39-43 (KJV).

Professor Roderick A. Finlayson taught me theology. Actually, he was supposed to be teaching me Greek, but when I went to meet with the retired professor I would begin by asking him questions about what I did not understand in the Bible. On many a winter's evening I would walk down to his house, and if it was raining he would open the door to me with a broad smile and in his croaky voice ask, 'Will ye no come in out of the wet? As the whale said to Jonah!' or some similar quip. I loved him as a father.

With that little introduction perhaps you can understand why I was slow to answer a question he had for me once: 'What were the first words of the New Testament to be written down?' I knew him well enough to know that the obvious answers would be proved wrong. The Gospels were written after the epistles so Matthew would certainly be the wrong answer. One of the Pauline epistles perhaps? But which one? Galatians? Well, that was my best guess. I might as well have gone with Matthew. It was just as wrong. So, what were the first words of the New Testament to be written down? The question is simple, of course, when you know the answer. The very first words of the New Testament to be written down were the words pinned to the cross above the head of our lovely Lord: 'This is the King of the Jews.' The disciples, with the exception of John the beloved disciple, were scattered and the last thing on their minds was writing the Gospels to bear witness to the Christ! As for Paul, he wasn't even converted yet. No, the first words were the words of the inscription, written if not by the hand then by the order of Pontius Pilate.

Just another quip from the sharp mind of Professor Finlayson? I looked at him quizzically and that broad smile told me he knew he had me hooked. 'So,' I asked, 'what's the significance of that?' Knowing that there was more to come.

He then began to expound on the dying thief on the cross.

If we compare the Gospel accounts, it would appear that initially both thieves railed against and mocked Christ in his agony. But at some point one of them either read the inscription or had it read to him. He certainly understood its content and better still had responded in faith to its clear message. It was the whole New Testament to that point and it spoke of the kingship of Christ. The dying thief, at least according to Professor Finlayson, had read the whole of the New Testament and was converted by it! Better still, he was prepared to act on it, 'Lord, remember me when you come in your kingdom.' Now that is faith. Who saw Jesus as king? The only disciple at the foot of the cross was John, and there is no evidence that even he beholding his noble Master saw him as a king. Cleopas on the road to Emmaus thought it was all over. Their hopes were dashed. The Pharisees or the Roman soldiers? Did they see King Jesus nailed to a cross? The passers-by on their way into Jerusalem? Did they see him as King Jesus? The only person who unmistakably saw Jesus as king was the penitent thief.

In a wonderful economy of words Scripture tells us a lot about his conversion. The penitent thief rebuked the other criminal, asking him did he not fear God. He knew that shortly, no matter how reluctantly, he would be standing before the ultimate judgment seat. He did more than that. He confessed himself to be rightly condemned. If he had no excuse to make in this life he certainly would have none in the life to come. When judgment came he would yield to it.

He did more. He acknowledged the moral perfection of Christ and started witnessing to his fellow criminal. 'This man has done nothing wrong!' Having explained to me the message of the gospel, and how it was received and understood by the thief on the cross, and how he alone saw Christ as king, confessed his sins, saw himself before God as he really was, my heart as well as my head was ready to hear what the thief had to say to Jesus. So simple! So eloquent! So moving! 'Lord, remember me when you come in your kingdom.'

Here is the humble petition of a sinner awakened by the gospel. The eye of flesh saw someone being executed like a common criminal. The eye of faith saw the King and he addressed him as such. His petition was filled with humble faith. He sought no easing of his painful burden, no escape from the justice he deserved. Only that this one who had done no wrong would remember him. And more, that though he had no hopes for himself, he was assured that Jesus would enter into his kingdom. It was a plea, 'Spare a thought for me. Just remember me, if you would.'

Now at this point, perhaps we should stop and ask ourselves what we would have asked Jesus for? A place in his kingdom. That would have been bold. What had the thief done to deserve that? A life of crime is hardly thought to be the best way to solicit God's favourable attention.

But what was Jesus' response? I hope your minds are

already attuned to the fact that *God is always better than we can imagine*. Yes, there would be a place for the thief in the kingdom of Christ Jesus. Perhaps he would find him a place as a gate keeper. How infinitely better that would be for the thief than his present circumstances. Perhaps an even bolder request would be to raise him to a position of some responsibility—to be granted some means by which he could serve.

But how does Jesus respond to this humble penitent soul? 'Truly!' says Jesus, staking his reputation for honesty and faithfulness behind the statement, 'You shall be with me in Paradise.'

We need to stop for a moment and reflect on what Jesus was actually promising. Let us not simply pass by the word 'Paradise' as though it were a synonym for heaven—wonderful and glorious though such a promise would have been. Think of a Middle Eastern king such as Nebuchadnezzar of Babylon or Artaxerxes of Persia. He would have been surrounded by courtiers and petitioners and all the matters associated with running a great earthly kingdom. There were times when the weighty responsibilities became so heavy that the king was in need of relief. At such times he would retire to his private garden where only a select few might enter. It was a place that the king went to relax with his intimate friends. One can imagine shady trees, water fountains, and flowers with their beauty and fragrance to delight the senses. That private garden of the king was called Paradise. And it was in Paradise that Jesus promised to see the thief again.

I sometimes wonder if the first person to enter heaven in the Old Testament was the victim of murder and the first person to enter heaven in the New was himself a murderer. That's speculation of course, but what is not, is that Jesus answered the request of the penitent thief exceeding abundantly above what he could ask or even think.

For further reflection:

1. What was the penitent thief able to promise Jesus he would do?

2. What was the promise Jesus made to the penitent thief?

3. What is your hope for eternity?

Meditation 22

It Was Better for You that I Was Not There

Now Jesus loved Martha and her sister and Lazarus. So, when he heard that Lazarus was ill, he stayed two days longer in the place where he was. Then after this he said to the disciples, 'Let us go to Judea again.' The disciples said to him, 'Rabbi, the Jews were just now seeking to stone you, and are you going there again?' Jesus answered, 'Are there not twelve hours in the day? If anyone walks in the day, he does not stumble, because he sees the light of this world. But if anyone walks in the night, he stumbles, because the light is not in him.' After saying these things, he said to them, 'Our friend Lazarus has fallen asleep, but I go to awaken him.' The disciples said to him, 'Lord, if he has fallen asleep, he will recover.' Now Jesus had spoken of his death, but they thought that he meant taking rest in sleep. Then Jesus told them plainly, 'Lazarus has died, and for your sake I am glad that I was not there,

so that you may believe. But let us go to him.'
So Thomas, called the Twin, said to his fellow
disciples, 'Let us also go, that we may die with
him.' — John 11:5-16.

My son has a picture of Lazarus on his cell phone. Don't
ask me why. It's a picture taken of a stone coffin found in
an ancient church in the south of France. It has to be said,
Lazarus does not look very happy. According to legend,
after Jesus raised him from the dead, he never smiled
again. I have no idea whether that legend is true or not,
but it does sound plausible. After all, if you had tasted
the bliss of heaven for even just a few days, returning to
earth must have been rather disappointing, even if you
were a wealthy man like Lazarus and had what the world
would describe as 'everything to live for.'

But I am getting ahead of myself. I would like to begin
the story at the point when Jesus heard that Lazarus was
sick. Jesus loved Lazarus and his two sisters, Mary and
Martha. So the response of Jesus is puzzling, or at least
it was to his disciples on that day. Instead of rushing
back to Bethany and healing his friend, Jesus delayed
his departure. The disciples seemed to have come up
with their own explanation: not long before this the
Jews had tried to stone Jesus, so obviously Jesus wasn't
going to go back and risk his life for Lazarus. But just
when the disciples thought they had it all worked out,
Jesus surprised them by saying that he was going back
to Bethany anyway.

Obviously this had them perplexed, so Jesus told them that Lazarus had fallen asleep. 'Well, that's good news,' they said, and if I might paraphrase their response, 'Sleep will give his body time to heal from whatever made him sick, so glad to hear it!'

'Lazarus is dead,' is the reply of Jesus. Not such good news after all.

It's at this point that I want to put in a word for Thomas—doubting Thomas, as he is often described. It has to be admitted that he earned the title. After all he did say, 'Unless I see in his hands the mark of the nails, and place my finger into the mark of the nails, and place my hand into his side, I will never believe.' Sounds like a lot of doubt to me. But as someone else observed, 'The evil that men do lives after them, the good is oft interred with their bones.' So while recognizing that we are not giants of the faith ourselves, let's also recognize that Thomas has something to say at this point too.

Thomas, as did the other disciples, remembered that there was an attempt on Jesus' life and expects that if they returned to Bethany, which was just a short walk from Jerusalem, the attempt might be turned into a reality. He also expected that those who were seeking Jesus' life will also want to snuff out the disciples, leaving no trace. There doesn't seem to be the same boldness that Peter was going to display when he later declared that he was willing to go to prison and to death. When Thomas says 'Let us also go, that we may die with him,' there is more a sense of resignation to the inevitable. But at least

Thomas is willing to go, even at the cost of his life. So let's give him credit so far as it goes.

On the other hand part of the curiosity of the situation, apart from the unusual circumstances, is that Jesus declared quite bluntly that for the disciples' sake he was actually glad that he was not there! Now think about what Jesus was saying to them. A couple of days beforehand, Jesus had received word that his friend Lazarus was lying seriously ill. But instead of going at once he delayed until Lazarus was dead. Then he declared to them that Lazarus was dead, and that he was glad for their sake that he was not there. It really sounds quite un-Jesus-like.

But do we trust that if Jesus does not speak or act as we think he should it must be that he has something better in mind? Perhaps there is more about Thomas with which we can identify than we care to admit: an air of resignation rather than faith in the wisdom of God.

But even when we don't understand, or when we think that we do but don't really, the safest place is to follow along in the company of Jesus.

As Jesus approached the home, Martha, ever the one who had to be up and doing, rushed out to meet Jesus. Her words were filled with confidence and yet tinged with rebuke, 'Lord, if you had been here my brother would not have died!'

'Your brother will rise again,' assures Jesus.

'I know he will rise again in the resurrection at the last day.'

'I am the resurrection and the life. He who believes in me will live, even though he dies, and whosoever lives and believes in me, will never die. Do you believe this?'

'Yes, Lord.'

Jesus has given Martha an assurance that her brother will rise again. She has received it with faith but placed the promise out of reach at some point in the future, who knows when? Spurgeon told a story to illustrate how so often we postpone the blessing in our thinking.

A soldier approaching the end of his days was being cared for by a widow. Shortly before he died he brought out a colourful piece of paper and gave it to the widow as an expression of his thanks for all she had done. After the soldier died, the widow much taken with the piece of paper had it framed and placed on the wall. Some years later a visitor questioned the widow wondering why she had such a high value bank note framed on the wall! She had received the gift from the soldier but not recognizing it as a foreign bank note had failed to turn it into the coin of the realm so that she might take her ease.

How many promises of God have we received, admired, and examined, and then consigned to some indeterminate future without turning the promise into the 'coin of the realm'—something we can use today?

Jesus had promised that Lazarus would rise. Martha didn't doubt that he would but somehow it wasn't really relevant to her present needs and sorrows. Jesus had told his disciples that he was glad for their sakes that he was not with Lazarus when he was sick. Here would be an unmistakable declaration of Jesus' power and more. Before their very eyes he would illustrate for them what he meant when he declared that he was himself the resurrection and the life.

If Jesus had returned when first he heard of Lazarus' illness, Mary, Martha, and the disciples would not have had this mighty demonstration of Jesus' power and authority. He was not only able to heal the sick, he is able to raise the dead. And is that not the testimony of everyone who believes in Christ: I was dead and Christ has raised me! I have life. No, better than that, I have eternal life! No, better than that, Jesus came to give me life in all its abundance. He is truly better than I can imagine.

But back to Martha. Martha returned to tell her sister Mary that Jesus had arrived. She in turn greeted him with exactly the same words, 'Lord, if you had been here my brother would not have died.'

What happened next is really quite curious. 'When Jesus saw her weeping, and the Jews who had come with her also weeping, he was deeply moved in his spirit and greatly troubled.' Now why would Jesus be 'deeply moved' and 'greatly troubled'? After all, he knew what he was about to do. In just a few minutes Lazarus would be standing before Mary and Martha alive again. Their sorrow would be at an end and their tears all gone. No need to be deeply moved then. No need to be greatly troubled. But he was.

To begin unravelling this we need to think his thoughts after him. Jesus had raised the conversation to the level of eternal realities, but neither Martha nor Mary had found the comfort in that which they should have. It is obvious when Martha, the first to speak again, responded to Jesus' command to roll away the stone. She said that it was probably not a good idea because Lazarus had been dead four days. Some of our English translations try to tone down what Martha said by removing the subject, 'there will be a bad odour.' The KJV is, I think, less subtle and more accurate, 'by this time he stinketh.'

But why was Jesus so deeply moved? I don't think the Jews understood when they said, 'See how he loved him!' They, too, were focused on the there and then. Jesus saw more than just the death of his friend whom shortly he would see again. He saw much more.

When Socrates drank the cup of hemlock, he did not appear to show any great anxiety. Why, then, did Jesus cast himself in the dust of the earth and why was his sweat like great drops of blood falling to the ground when faced with his own death? Was Socrates made of sterner stuff than Jesus? Perish the thought! When he gazed into 'the cup' he saw the awful consequences of sin in death and being separated from his Father. Socrates saw no such thing. As Jesus stood at the tomb of Lazarus, his friend whom he loved, he was confronted with the awful consequences of sin for man, and he mourned deeply. Death is the hideous result of our rebellion against God.

The man of sorrows wept not only over Lazarus but over Jerusalem. There are few more affecting passages in Scripture than the description: 'O Jerusalem, Jerusalem, the city that kills the prophets and stones those who are sent to it! How often would I have gathered your children together as a hen gathers her brood under her wings, and you would not!'

Weeping over a friend we can understand. *But God is always better than we can imagine.* Jesus weeps over those who had stoned the very messengers God had sent to call them back to himself.

Don't think of God as the Judge who is always ready to cast sinners into a lost eternity. Jesus 'desires all people to be saved and to come to the knowledge of the truth.' When humanity stands before the Lord Jesus Christ at the last day for judgment, he will cast no one into hell over whom he has not wept.

For further reflection:

1. Does God have a purpose in delaying an answer to prayer?

2. Who feels the sorrow of death more than you ever have or will?

3. What were you when God commended his love to you by sending his Son to die for you?

Meditation 23

The Spirit of Adoption

So then, brothers, we are debtors, not to the flesh, to live according to the flesh. For if you live according to the flesh you will die, but if by the Spirit you put to death the deeds of the body, you will live. For all who are led by the Spirit of God are sons of God. For you did not receive the spirit of slavery to fall back into fear, but you have received the Spirit of adoption as sons, by whom we cry, 'Abba! Father!' The Spirit himself bears witness with our spirit that we are children of God, and if children, then heirs — heirs of God and fellow heirs with Christ, provided we suffer with him in order that we may also be glorified with him. — Romans 8:12-17.

You have to admire those who adopt a child. It is usually undertaken only with great expense and considerable effort. I am staggered by those who have been willing to go to the Ukraine or China or the Philippines in order to deal sometimes with the helpful officials who have seemed more interested in cashing in on a big heart than on relieving the distress of a child. Adopting into a family does, however, provide us with a biblical picture of an aspect of God's great mercy. But let us start at the beginning.

We will not begin to grasp the greatness of what God has done for us unless we understand from what he has saved us. I suspect that is the weakness of much preaching today when the emphasis is on 'being saved' with hardly a nod in the direction of from what God is saving us. It is almost as though the *sinner* (who is not called that of course) — it is almost as though the 'seeker' is curious about what it means to be a Christian and is told it is like winning the lottery, only much better. Well, I am not going to argue with that. After all, *God is always better than you can imagine!* My issue is that we can function quite adequately, and, of course, most of us do, without winning the lottery. And a lot of people will no doubt respond that they are quite happy for *you* to have Jesus in your life, but *they* can get by, have got by, quite comfortably without him, and do not really feel the need for a change. That is why the sort of preaching that asks the inquirer if he has 'tried Jesus' is at best very inadequate. It does not recognize the depths of our need.

Jesus is not to be thought of as the last lonely student at the Prom who is desperately hoping that someone will ask him to dance!

Let us get biblical! Though most of us think (with good reason) of Romans as being Paul's greatest letter, I would suggest the application of the gospel is even clearer in his letter to the Ephesians.

Take a look at the opening of Ephesians chapter 2. It is as though Paul has gone down to the local art store and has asked for the very darkest blacks available. He wants to paint a picture. This is what a person without Christ is like. This is what you were like before Christ saved you, or what you are like right now if you are not his. Don't turn away. Hear how God depicts the sinner without Christ.

> And you were dead in your trespasses and sins in which you once walked, following the course of this world, following the prince of the power of the air, the spirit that is now at work in the sons of disobedience—among whom we all once lived in the passions of our flesh, carrying out the desires of the body and the mind, and were by nature children of wrath, like the rest of mankind.

Dead! Not a bit of a head cold that affects our thinking in some ways. Not seriously ill. Not on life support, but dead! We followed the prince of the power of the air—the one who is at work in the sons of disobedience. We lived in the passions of our flesh. We carried out the desires of the body. We carried out the desires of the mind. We were just like everyone else. By nature we were the children of wrath.

Each clause seems darker than the one that came before. It is unrelieved in its misery until two glorious words break the downward spiral of darkness: 'But God ...'! The light of the gospel shatters the gloom and despair.

Be the darkness never so great the piercing light of God can cut through.

How does Paul begin to tell us of the benefits of God's work of grace in the gospel? In the next paragraph, Paul uses the illustration of citizenship. Formerly we were estranged or alienated, but now we are citizens. Perhaps you will recall that Paul was conscious of the fact that he was a citizen of 'no mean city' and used his Roman citizenship on more than one occasion to his advantage. It gave him privileges, and he used those privileges. What privileges do we have as citizens of the kingdom of heaven that we forget about? My old British passport states, 'Her Britannic Majesty's Secretary of State requests in the name of Her Majesty all those whom it may concern to allow the bearer to pass freely without let or hindrance, and to afford the bearer such assistance and protection as may be necessary.' Will the King of kings demand less for his subjects?

But that illustration isn't really good enough, is it? Not according to Paul. For *God is always better than we can imagine*. It is not just that we are citizens, but that we are *sons*. We've been adopted into God's family. We have the privilege of calling God, 'Our Father.' When Jesus taught his disciples to pray, the very first lesson was to call God 'Father.' If our earthly parents know how to give us good gifts how much more will our heavenly Father give us the Holy Spirit when we ask? If God did not spare his own Son, but gave him up for us all, how will he not also, along with him, graciously give us all things?

So there we have it! Not only citizenship with all its privileges, but adopted into his family. But *God is always better than we can imagine.* What more is there beyond mere citizenship and being adopted into the family of the King of kings? There is more. He has given us the 'Spirit of adoption.'

Perhaps you have known of situations where an adoption undertaken with love and thoughtfulness has not worked out. The tensions between the child and the adoptive parents are never far from the surface, and periodically explode with the words, 'You're not my real father!' Do you see what God gives us? He gives us the 'Spirit of adoption' which enables us to cry, 'Abba, Father!' Once I was alienated from God. I was dead in my sins. But God, who is rich in mercy raised me from the dead, gave me citizenship in heaven and as though that were not enough, adopted me into his family, and more, he gave me the Spirit of adoption enabling me to cry out, 'Abba, Father!'

How good is the God we adore!

For further reflection:

1. What was your spiritual state before you were made a child of God?

2. What are the different ways God has changed your status?

3. Is there more to you status than you realize even now?

Meditation 24

All Things Work Together for Good to Them that Love God

Likewise the Spirit helps us in our weakness. For we do not know what to pray for as we ought, but the Spirit himself intercedes for us with groanings too deep for words. And he who searches hearts knows what is the mind of the Spirit, because the Spirit intercedes for the saints according to the will of God. And we know that for those who love God all things work together for good, for those who are called according to his purpose. For those whom he foreknew he also predestined to be conformed to the image of his Son, in order that he might be the first-born among many brothers. And those whom he predestined he also called, and those whom he called he also justified, and those whom he justi-fied he also glorified. —Romans 8:26-30.

'Man is born to trouble as the sparks fly upwards.' What that quotation from Job 5:7 lacks in cheeriness it makes up for with realism. We shouldn't be surprised. If the world hates us, then know that it hated our Master before us (John 15:18, 19). It's not that he didn't warn us: 'In the world you will have tribulation' (John 16:33). It shouldn't come as a shock to us that there are more than thirty psalms in which the psalmist cried out for help in a day of trouble.

What does come as a surprise is encountering preachers who seem to be saying the exact opposite of what the Bible clearly states. If Jesus tells us plainly that in this world we will have trouble, then I am at a loss to know how anyone can give an assurance to his hearers or readers that we can have our best life now. I don't even know why this would be deemed good news. Think about it. If we have our best life now then whatever comes afterwards must necessarily not be our best life. The logic is that heaven will actually be a downgrade.

The other possibility is, of course, that there will be those who will go to a lost eternity who did indeed have their best life now. But it will be little comfort to them to know that they frittered away every opportunity to hear and respond to the gospel in the pursuit of a temporary blessing. But that seems to be the meaning of the full-size hoarding at the side of the interstate telling travellers that 'God wants you winning in life!'

Before we can climb to the heights of what God has planned, we will have to take a few more steps down into the depths. Whatever some preachers may or may not be saying or meaning with their promises of health and wealth, the straightforward implication of Scripture is that life will not necessarily get better by becoming a Christian. Those who say otherwise are doing you a great disservice. When life doesn't get better as promised, then those who have listened to such preachers will inevitably find fault with themselves. But just take a look at that remarkable event when Jesus came to the disciples walking on the water.

Jesus had fed the five thousand. He had given them bread and fish, but he also nourished the multitude with the word of God before dismissing the people and going up on the hillside to pray. But it's what he said in regard to the disciples that I find most intriguing: 'He made his disciples get into the boat and go before him to the other side, to Bethsaida.' He *made* them. He didn't simply make a suggestion or agree to one of theirs, but 'he made them.'

When the storm arose they were exactly where he had told them to be. The five thousand were no doubt safely tucked up in bed, but the disciples fought against wind and waves. But it was the wind and waves which he had *made* them face. Don't think that by following Jesus you will have gentle breezes, blue skies, and plain sailing. The disciples didn't get that, and neither will you.

Well, that's not particularly encouraging, now is it? It really depends on where you are looking for encouragement, doesn't it? When were the disciples safe? When Jesus stilled the wind and waves? Of course, but were they not safe when he was in the boat and the wind was still blowing fiercely? Of course they were. What about when

Jesus came walking towards them across the sea? Yes, even then too. Take a look at these verses and tell if the disciples were safe when we read, 'he saw that they were making headway painfully, for the wind was against them' (Mark 6:48). Where was he at the time? The Bible tells us 'he was alone on the land (6:45). Sure, but where was he in another sense? That's a little bit obscure as questions go, so let me tell you simply; 'he went up the mountain to pray.' He was in his Father's presence. So where is Jesus right now? I don't mean where was he when the events of the story took place, but where is right now as you sit reading this book or hearing someone read it to you? Stop a minute and think about the answer? *Where is he?* The Bible answers that question too. He has ascended up to the Father's right hand (cf. Acts 2:33; Col. 3:1; Heb. 1:3). But I have another question for you. We know where he is, but *what is he doing?* I mean right now, what is Jesus doing? The Bible answers that one too. He always lives to make intercession for us (Heb. 7:25).

In the midst of the storm let us take our comfort from what God promises us, and not from what he does not. He does not promise us a life of ease, but he does promise that his Son, Jesus Christ, will sustain us with his prayers. Do you have friends praying for you? I do. I had an email from a friend just this morning to tell me he was praying for me and for the writing of this book. But with no disrespect to the dear friend praying for me, it is infinitely better to have the Son of God praying for me. And that's what he is doing right now.

So we have taken some steps down into the valley of troubles, and have recognized that in this world we will have trouble, and some of these troubles will come on us not because we are being disobedient, but because we are being obedient. It will be harder, not easier, for us because we are followers of the Lord.

But I think we are just about at the bottom, and now we can start to make the ascent. And this is where our text from Romans chapter 8 comes in. It's a text which has comforted every generation of believers since Paul first sent it to the saints in Rome. 'And we know that for those who love God all things work together for good, for those who are called according to his purpose.'

How many times have we taken hold of that verse in the midst of some profound catastrophe when all seems lost in the gloom? God, the one who cannot lie, has promised us that if we belong to him, then whatever difficulties we face, whatever sorrow, whatever distress in whatever shape it comes — 'all things will work together for good.'

There are some very simple and straightforward applications of this verse. *God is in control*. Whatever the darkness of the hour, God has a purpose and that purpose is to do me good. So the first question I need to ask myself is, 'Am I trusting God?' Trusting him in his wisdom, in his mercy, in his goodness, in his tenderness towards me.

Many years ago I was part of a children's club. We took some children swimming. I think it was the first time some had ever been in a swimming pool. The shallow end was not at all deep, but there was one small child who wrapped herself around me. When I waded out just a little further she clung ever tighter. And the further I got away from the edge, the more she tightened her grip. She was never in any danger. I had a firm hold of her. That did not mean she did not grow anxious as the water got deeper. So our Father holds on to us, and though we may grow anxious, we are really safe in our Father's arms, and need to learn to trust him more.

But there is another lesson in this wonderful verse. *Every struggle has a purpose.* The other side of the coin is that there are no struggles that we as Christians face that are without purpose. Now develop that thought a little further. The burden of your sorrow is not one bit heavier than it needs to be, nor will it last one moment longer than it needs to, in order for God to accomplish his purpose in you and for you.

How could it be otherwise? When God has accomplished his purpose, he will remove the affliction. It was Professor Donald Macleod who drew my attention to the words of Isaiah 53:9: 'they made his grave with the wicked and with a rich man in his death, although he had done no violence, and there was no deceit in his mouth.' We see that prophecy of Isaiah fulfilled at the time of the death of Jesus. He was crucified between two thieves, but buried in the expensive tomb, hollowed out of the hillside, that belonged to Joseph of Arimathea. It was as though God would not permit his Son to be humiliated in his poverty for one more moment longer than necessary, hence 'with a rich man in his death.' And we can be assured of this, God will snatch us away from tribulation just as soon as it can be done.

But there is more, for *God is always better than we can imagine.*

Though we are tempted to focus on the verse that brings so much comfort in assuring us that 'all things,' that's right, *all things* work together for good, for those who are called according to the purposes of God, we should read on to the next verse. It's in the next verse that we are told what that great purpose is. Here it is: 'For those whom he foreknew he also predestined to be conformed to the image of his Son, in order that he might be the firstborn among many brothers.'

The great purpose of God and the reason why he does more than merely permit difficulties to come our way is to conform us to the image of his Son. He is making us more and more like his Son. Who else, dear believing friend, would you want to be more like? Have you never felt the pain of a word you knew brought shame on his lovely name because you were known to be his? Or an action? In our better moments all who know Christ want to be more like him. And that is God's wonderful purpose.

When my dear friend, and father in the Lord, Professor Roderick Finlayson, was taken up to be with the Saviour he loved and served, Professor Douglas Macmillan preached from the Psalms. The sermon was from Psalm 17: 'As for me, I shall behold your face in righteousness; when I awake, I shall be satisfied with your likeness.'

There in the Old Testament David sets before us the hope of all who love the Lord. We fall asleep in this world to wake in his nearer presence. As Professor Finlayson told me, 'We do not so much as change our environment.'

The hoarding had it tragically wrong. It's not so much that God wants us winning in *life*: he wants us winning in *death*.

'When I awake, I shall be satisfied with your likeness.' Amen.

For further reflection:

1. Does God promise you a stress-free life?

2. Do the difficulties you face come to you for a reason?

3. What is the good for which God is working in your life?

Meditation 25

Christmas All Over Again: The Gift of the Holy Spirit

But I have said these things to you, that when their hour comes you may remember that I told them to you. 'I did not say these things to you from the beginning, because I was with you. But now I am going to him who sent me, and none of you asks me, 'Where are you going?' But because I have said these things to you, sorrow has filled your heart. Nevertheless, I tell you the truth: it is to your advantage that I go away, for if I do not go away, the Helper will not come to you. But if I go, I will send him to you. And when he comes, he will convict the world concerning sin and righteousness and judgment: concerning sin, because they do not believe in me; concerning righteousness, because I go to the Father, and you will see me no longer; concerning judgment, because the ruler of this world is judged.

—John 16:4-11.

I serve a congregation of honest, hard-working, straight-forward, and very generous folk who have no difficulty in speaking their mind. For some that description will be enough to tell you that they come from a Dutch background. Sometimes they might perplex me, but not as much, I'm sure, as I perplex them! That's because in spite of the fact that we have different backgrounds we are still family, and I love the people whom the Lord has been pleased to call me to pastor, and I have so many tokens of their love towards me that I do not doubt but that the love is mutual.

When I visit their homes I have often heard stories of how grand-parents or great grand-parents left The Netherlands to come to the United States of America. Those must have been solemn times indeed. Most would have crossed the Atlantic by ship with the knowledge that it was most unlikely that they would ever be able to return to their homeland. They left behind all that was familiar, in many cases taking leave of parents and other members of family without much hope of seeing them again this side of glory. What struck me most was the fact that those final farewells were undertaken in the context of worship, and would often conclude with the singing of a psalm, often Psalm 121.

It may be that not everyone who crossed the Atlantic brought such a firm love for the Lord and his word but enough of them did to bequeath a lively inheritance in the faith. I know because I serve their grandchildren and great grandchildren. I also join with them in desiring and praying that a generation yet unborn, should the Lord tarry, will also declare a confidence in the Lord in joy and also, if need be, in parting.

Well, those who left Europe for the States most likely had some anxious moments. Perhaps at times they may have wondered if all would indeed be well. As we think about such a solemn parting, it may give us something of an insight into the anxious thoughts that filled the hearts and minds of the disciples on a night long ago.

It's not that Jesus hadn't tried to prepare them for his departure. As the authors of the Gospels make clear, Jesus had often told them what would happen to him in Jerusalem. But we have a sometimes surprising capacity for not hearing what we don't want to hear. It was only as Jesus was on the very brink of being taken from his disciples that the solemnity of the hour seemed to weigh heavily on them. Jesus, on the other, was far from being in denial. He knew all too well what lay ahead of him. Anyone else would have been preoccupied with his own concerns, but Jesus' thoughts were for his disciples.

How gently does he open his word of encouragement! 'Let not your hearts be troubled.' I am comforted by those words as though Jesus were in the room speaking to me right now. I know of course that he is, but you understand my meaning. My theology tells me—by which I simply mean the word of God convinces me in my head—that I am in my Father's hand, and that 'I am sure that neither death nor life, nor angels nor rulers, nor things present nor things to come, nor powers, or height nor depth, nor anything else in all creation, will be able to separate [me] from the love of God in Christ Jesus our Lord' (Rom. 8:38, 39). The saints in heaven may be more sanctified but they are not more secure. But what I know in my head does not always make its way into my heart. Now Jesus would have grounds for chiding me for my lack of trust. He would be right to do so. He could have chided the disciples, but he didn't. When he found Peter, James and John asleep after he had asked them to watch with him in prayer, there was no rebuke, but a seeking of an excuse, 'The spirit indeed is willing but the flesh is weak' (Mark 14:38). Such is the Master we serve.

So Jesus tells them not to be troubled and then proceeds to give them reasons why they should not be discouraged. He tells them where he is going, what he is going to do, and what his plans are for the future. He is going to his Father. In the King James Version, Jesus tells them that in his Father's house there are many mansions. He tells them, 'And if I go and prepare a place for you, I will come again, and receive you unto myself, that where I am, there ye may be also.'

Long after that night, the words are still heavy with promise, but it is much easier to grasp the promise after the event and because we were not with Jesus in the company of the disciples. Neither have we been with them in the school of Christ. For three years they had been enrolled in a travelling seminary, being taught and pastored by Christ himself. They were about to graduate Masters of Divinity but they were alarmed that the talk now was of their noble Master and lovely Lord being taken from their midst.

As we look back on that evening it is not to condemn the disciples. I don't think for one moment I would have fared better. In fact, I think I would have fared much worse. I would not have wished to see that time come to an end. I would have wished that the ministry of Jesus on earth could go on for ever; to see others healed or raised, to hear him teach and explain the very word of God, and best of all to hear him pray. 'Don't tell me, Jesus, you are leaving! That's *not* what I want to hear. And don't tell me that it is better for you to leave. How could it possibly be better than having you here, right here, right now?'

'Nevertheless,' says Jesus, 'I tell you the truth: it is to your advantage that I go away, for if I do not go away, the Helper will not come to you. But if I go, I will send him to you' (John 16:7).

So, it was to the disciples' advantage for Jesus to go away. How likely is it the disciples saw the advantage? Perhaps I should not speak for them, but I don't think I would have seen it as an advantage. But *God is always better than we can imagine.*

When Jesus ascended into the presence of his Father, he took my humanity with him. The sacrifice he had made was accepted. The work of redemption he had undertaken was completed. Now that is certainly to my advantage!

But there is more, Jesus promised the gift of the Holy Spirit: the Comforter. He is given to the people of God in a way that was not true of the Old Testament Church.

He searches out the deep things of God. He helps us to understand what we could not if left to ourselves. The things of God are 'spiritually discerned,' and the natural person does not receive them (1 Cor. 2:14). That's you and me without the illumination of the Holy Spirit.

But there is one further great blessing. His Spirit bears witness with my spirit that I am a child of God (Rom. 8:16). I don't have access to the Lamb's book of life (Rev. 21:27). I am not able infallibly to discern who is a believer and who is not. No doubt I will be astonished as to whom I will see in heaven and by the same token those whom I will not. Now many a believer has been wracked with doubt and in a state of perpetual fear regarding his or her salvation. If you, dear reader, are such a one, let me address a few words to you.

As you think of your own parents, did they have a desire to assure you with their every embrace that you were more dear to them than life itself? If they did not, did you wish that they did? Which sounds nearer the ideal, the parent who never communicates any affection or the parent who hardly lets an opportunity pass to assure the child that he or she is loved and secure? And at which end of the spectrum do you expect to find your heavenly Father? To ask the question is to answer it. Do you suppose that your Father in heaven wants you to spend your time wondering and ever guessing if he loves you? You want to know the answer to that because you want his love. But why do you want his love? Because you love him. And why do you love him? We love because he first loved us.

> I know not why God's wondrous grace
> > To me he has made known;
> Or why, unworthy as I am,
> > He chose me for his own.

> *But I know whom I have believed,*
> > *And am persuaded that he is able*
> *To keep that which I've committed*
> > *Unto him against that day.*

That truly is the work of the Comforter.

For further reflection:

1. What advantage is it to you that Christ has ascended up into heaven?

2. What blessings come to you from the Comforter?

3. Do you think God wants you to be uncertain of His love?

Meditation 26

The Prayer of Stephen and the Conversion of Saul of Tarsus

Now when they heard these things they were enraged, and they ground their teeth at him. But he, full of the Holy Spirit, gazed into heaven and saw the glory of God, and Jesus standing at the right hand of God. And he said, 'Behold, I see the heavens opened, and the Son of Man standing at the right hand of God.' But they cried out with a loud voice and stopped their ears and rushed together at him. Then they cast him out of the city and stoned him. And the witnesses laid down their garments at the feet of a young man named Saul. And as they were stoning Stephen, he called out, 'Lord Jesus, receive my spirit.' And falling to his knees he cried out with a loud voice, 'Lord, do not hold this sin against them.' And when he had said this, he fell asleep. — Acts 7:54-60.

I love the Psalms. I hope you do, too. In fact there are some congregations that sing only psalms in worship.

They are known to be exclusive psalmodists because they sing psalms 'exclusively.' Historically, you would have been hard-pressed to find a congregation in Scotland, my native country, that sang anything but psalms for the first three hundred years after the Reformation. That's hardly a principled reason for singing just psalms, but the fact that the pressure to add hymns to the diet of church worship came from a visit to Scotland by Moody and Sankey, may not be seen by everyone too favourably.

Whether or not you are an exclusive psalmodist, the danger on the other side is ending up an exclusive hymnodist—you only sing hymns. If you think that isn't a problem, then think of how many services you have been in where you have not sung a psalm at all. Does that matter? It does if we want to be biblical. In Colossians Paul stated explicitly we should sing 'psalms, hymns and spiritual songs.' Our exclusive psalmody friends will tell us that these are three categories of psalms. Our non-exclusive psalmody friends are not convinced by that argument. What I have yet to hear argued is that we should not be singing psalms at all. The argument is only about whether we are permitted to sing something other than a psalm or not. So even if you are not an exclusive psalmodist, I don't think you can be an exclusive hymnodist, which is where most seem to end up.

So, I love the Psalms, and so should you. But now I have a confession to make. Among those psalms there are some which I find myself reluctant to apply in the way some would have me apply them. Now I love these brothers and have enormous respect for them, but neither my love nor my respect for them has convinced me that I should be praying the imprecatory Psalms—those are the Psalms which call down God's judgment, sometimes in a most graphic way, on those who stand opposed to the things of the Lord.

I have heard dear friends say that we should. I have read others arguing for their use both in learned articles and in books, and yet so far I have yet to be won over to the position. They are in Scripture and I honour them as part of God's revealed word, but while it is still the day of grace, I have not yet been able to bring myself to call down the anger of God on his enemies and mine. That day will come. Of that I have no doubt. It is not here yet, and while the Lord tarries, I cannot bring myself to ask for God's judgment to be visited even on the worst of sinners, for fear I would be condemning myself.

Whether or not we should be praying the imprecatory Psalms, I think a strong case can be made for them not being mandatory. Take, for example, Jesus on the cross.

There are some parts of Scripture that have an 'Exodus 3' feel about them. When Moses wandered across to see a burning bush that was not consumed, and met with God, he was told to take his shoes off because the ground he was walking on was holy ground. There are times when I am reading Scripture that I want to slip my shoes off too. The ground just seems to be holy.

When I read through the Gospel accounts of Jesus' death I feel like that. Jesus was nailed to a cross, and I know it was because of his love for me. Of course there was pain—more pain than I have ever known or ever hope to know. The method of execution was designed to inflict suffering. The weight of the body hanging on the arms would compress the lungs, making it difficult to breathe. In order to breathe the victim would have to push up on the nails fixing him through his hands (or wrists) and feet. That was until the pain became utterly unbearable, and the victim would slump down once more, until the need to breathe would start the cycle over again. It was a cycle that could easily continue for days (that's why Pontius Pilate was surprised to hear that Jesus was dead so soon, Mark 15:44), and sometimes weeks. The reason the soldiers came to break the legs of the two thieves was to stop them from being able to push themselves up to breathe, and to hasten their death.

The process of dying on a cross was cruel and painful. Now I don't want in any sense to minimize the agony of the cross, the physical agony that is; but that is not where the real focus of the Gospel accounts lies. Think about this when someone urges you to see a movie depicting the physical suffering of Christ. Quite aside from the violation of the second commandment forbidding the making of images of any member of the Trinity, such movies utterly miss the point.

There was an agony of the cross that went above and beyond the physical suffering of Christ. Jesus suffered this agony when he who knew no sin became sin for us. It was what he was undertaking in the presence of

God as he offered himself as a sacrifice on our behalf. The focus, therefore, is not on the physical pain of crucifixion. Others have been crucified, and others have endured great pain on crosses for longer periods than Jesus experienced. But only Christ was forsaken of his Father. As Professor Donald Macleod has said, no one was less prepared. That's a striking statement, isn't it? You and I know what it is to live without God. Sometimes, to our shame, we can live without communion with the Father for considerable stretches of time. What experience had Jesus ever had of being separated from the Father? Throughout endless ages the Father and the Son communed in all the fullness of infinite and eternal love. That communion was unbroken throughout Jesus' earthly ministry. That is, until the moment he became our great sin-bearer and the favour of his Father was withdrawn from him.

It was not, nor could it ever be the physical pain of crucifixion, but the spiritual agony of being separated from his Father that wrung from his lips that startling question, 'My God, my God, why have you forsaken me?' (Matt. 27:46).

It is important that we are as fully conscious of the context as finite sinners can be, to understand the weight of Jesus' prayer: 'Father, forgive them for they know not what they do' (Luke 23:34). Whatever tribulations we pass through cannot begin to compare with the suffering of Christ on the cross on whatever dimension we consider it. And yet, there in the midst of his agony he prayed for forgiveness, and not for the judgment of God to descend upon his cruel tormentors.

I believe that God did indeed most graciously answer that prayer from the cross. Around six weeks later the Spirit of God came on Peter, and he preached a powerful sermon on the death and resurrection of Christ. He didn't pull any punches either: 'this Jesus, whom *you* crucified.' These were the same people who had come to Jerusalem to celebrate the Passover and had called for Jesus to be crucified. As Peter preached, the Holy Spirit brought many under conviction and 3,000 were converted.

But what Jesus did in sovereign grace on the cross is not for us to imitate. We can't, after all, copy him dying for someone else's sins.

Yet that is where our text comes in. Stephen was clearly a most remarkable man. He is hardly spoken of in Scripture without it being pointed out that he was filled with the Holy Spirit. Perhaps it was just because he was so preeminently a man of God, that the great enemy of our souls made sure he was singled out to be the first martyr. Stephen made a marvellous defence of the faith but to no avail. There was an inevitability about the outcome.

Stephen was jostled and frog-marched outside. Men took off their cloaks so that they could more easily and forcefully hurl the rocks and stones that would kill him. As each rock made contact with him, shattering bone and causing the blood to flow, Stephen echoed the words of Jesus and asked the Lord to forgive them. It's important for us to note exactly what Stephen was saying. Stephen did not say that he was forgiving them. Sadly, we can hear that well-intentioned but mistaken sentiment expressed after some tragic shooting. The family of the victim go in front of the television cameras to tell the world that they forgive the perpetrator. But think that through. If the perpetrator is unrepentant, he will go to a lost eternity where God will bring on him the full weight of his justice. So though the family has forgiven him, God has not. Wouldn't that make the family more willing to forgive than God himself. Does that sound right?

But it is not Stephen who is doing the forgiving. He is asking God to do the forgiving, and when God does the forgiving we are on surer ground.

God does hear that prayer and answers it exceeding abundantly above all that we can ask or think. As the rocks crashed down on Stephen's head his prayer was for the forgiveness for those who wished to see him dead. There was a man in that crowd whose name is well known to us: Saul of Tarsus. Many years later he was to describe himself as the 'chief of sinners' (1 Tim. 1:15). God heard Stephen's prayer and answered it in a way that no one could possibly have imagined: the conversion and transformation of Saul of Tarsus into the Paul the Apostle to the Gentiles.

For further reflection:

1. Was anyone less prepared to be separated from the Father than Jesus?

2. Did the Father hear Jesus' prayer for those who tormented him?

3. How abundantly did God answer the prayer of Stephen?

Meditation 27

Creation Groaning:
Something Better than Heaven

For I consider that the sufferings of this present time are not worth comparing with the glory that is to be revealed to us. For the creation waits with eager longing for the revealing of the sons of God. For the creation was subjected to futility, not willingly, but because of him who subjected it, in hope that the creation itself will be set free from its bondage to decay and obtain the freedom of the glory of the children of God. For we know that the whole creation has been groaning together in the pains of childbirth until now. And not only the creation, but we ourselves, who have the firstfruits of the Spirit, groan inwardly as we wait eagerly for adoption as sons, the redemption of our bodies. For in this hope we were saved. Now hope that is seen is not hope. For who hopes for what he sees? But if we hope for what we do not see, we wait for it with patience. — Romans 8:18-25.

In the days of sail, ships would sometimes go into battle with their colours nailed to the mast. Why? If their colours, that is their flag was physically nailed to the mast it could not so easily be 'struck,' or taken down to signify surrender. In fact ships of the Royal Navy have what is known as a 'Battle Ensign' which is larger than the ensign they normally display so as to make sure that everyone knows to whom they belong.

Well, let me nail my colours to the mast when it comes to how I read and understand the opening chapters of Genesis. It seems to me the most natural reading of the creation account is to see God's work as taking place in six normal straightforward days.

Now I have no desire whatsoever to cause you offence, dear reader. It may be that you have come to a different conclusion, even if I do not understand how you reached it. I am certainly most willing to concede that there are those whose knowledge of Scripture greatly exceeds my own, who disagree with my position. I have no doubt that their knowledge of Scripture greatly exceeds my own, nor do I doubt that the intellectual faculties with which God has graced them are also abundantly greater than mine. Further, I will yield that their academic achievements and skills are unquestionably greater than mine. More, I am more than ready to concede that many who have held a position on this subject different to mine stand much closer to the throne of God than I will ever do. I am willing to make all and every concession to those who take a different position, but one thing I cannot do is say that I have been convinced by their arguments, when I have not.

On a very basic level, it does seem clear to me at least, that the original hearers would have understood Moses to have meant six days of normal length. Perhaps the dear brethren who take a different view might debate that, but when Moses tells us that we should work for six days and rest for one, he does so by saying that the Lord made the heavens and the earth in six days and rested for one. The basis for the working week seems to rest on a straightforward reading of Genesis 1.

But perhaps an even greater stumbling block for me is the implication for the Christ's atoning work.

That's a serious concern. Let me explain. If God did not create the world in six days of more or less the usual length, then the inevitable result, it seems to me, is that we are left with death before the fall. At least all those with whom I have had conversations about this matter who hold to a longer period of time have been willing to agree that that is indeed a consequence. Now when they talk about death before the fall, they do not mean to include man's death but the death of animals. We might suggest a couple of reasons for the death of animals. They might have died as a result of predators or because of disease. But if there is any extended period in the region of thousands if not millions of years, then during that time generations must have passed away. In a sense it doesn't matter if predators or disease removed them. God either has to look upon a lion taking down an antelope and tearing it apart, and declare that to be good, or watch an animal dying of cancer or some such debilitating sickness and likewise say that is good. Neither seems plausible.

But perhaps my friend who takes a different view of the creation account doesn't see animals tearing one another apart as problematic. Perhaps he can envisage God looking on 'nature red in tooth and claw' and pronouncing that to be good—just what he intended. I have to say it leaves me scratching my head.

But here is the greatest problem of all for me. What does such a view say about the atoning work of Jesus? If there was death before the fall, then the atoning work of Christ only has relevance for the death that came about as a result of sin; in other words, the atoning work of Christ only has reference to the death that came about as a result of man's fall, and in that scenario, it is only death for men for which Christ came to atone.

That does seem to me to limit the atoning work of Christ in a way that is inconsistent with Scripture. According to Paul in Romans, it is not only believers who are awaiting the final consummation of Christ's redeeming work, but the whole of creation too.

That surely is a fuller understanding of the cosmic level on which Christ's atonement works. In such a world I can understand how a lion can lie down with a lamb.

And that brings me to the application of creation and Christ's work of redemption. We are accustomed to thinking that after this life we will, as believers, go to heaven. And that is the final blessing for which we long.

So many of our songs speak in such a way. I remember singing a chorus with the line 'heaven is the haven that I am going to.' It came as a surprise to me, even a shock, that heaven was not actually what Scripture teaches us to hope for. I've seen the same shock on the faces of other warm-hearted believers who have never considered that heaven is not meant to be what fixes our attention.

So let me state it plainly, God promises something better than heaven! What on earth could be better than heaven? I choose my words carefully. We were never intended to be disembodied spirits. God has promised something better than heaven itself for his people. When Christ comes again in all his glory, the graves will yield up their dead and the souls which have been with him in heaven shall be reunited with their bodies. 'What is sown is perishable; what is raised is imperishable. It is sown in dishonour; it is raised in glory. It is sown in weakness; it is raised in power. It is sown a natural body; it is raised a spiritual body.'

We most certainly can say with Paul that for me to live is Christ and to die is gain. But *God is always better than we can imagine*. We are not snatched from the world and separated forever from our physical bodies. God has promised to redeem creation itself, not just to pay the penalty of sin, staggering though that is. God has promised to redeem and renew the whole of creation. The sky will be rolled back as a scroll (Rev. 6:14). There will be a new heaven and a new earth, and in that new earth there will be no sun nor moon, for the Lord himself shall be its light. How glorious will the new creation be! Better than we can imagine!

For further reflection:

1. What is all creation waiting for?

2. What will be better than heaven?

3. Can you think of some ways in which the new earth will be better than the old one?

Meditation 28

More Than Just Loved in Heaven

And you were dead in the trespasses and sins in which you once walked, following the course of this world, following the prince of the power of the air, the spirit that is now at work in the sons of disobedience—among whom we all once lived in the passions of our flesh, carrying out the desires of the body and the mind, and were by nature children of wrath, like the rest of mankind. But God, being rich in mercy, because of the great love with which he loved us, even when we were dead in our trespasses, made us alive together with Christ- by grace you have been saved—and raised us up with him and seated us with him in the heavenly places in Christ Jesus, so that in the coming ages he might show the immeasurable riches of his grace in kindness toward us in Christ Jesus. For by grace you have been saved through faith. And this is not your own doing; it is the gift of God, not a result of works, so that no one may boast.—Ephesians 2:1-9.

What is the best known verse in the Bible? My guess would be John 3:16: 'For God so loved the world that he gave his only Son that whoever believes in him should not perish but have eternal life.' It's not that I have ever sat down to memorize it but I seemed to have heard it so many times that I didn't need to. I suspect that I am not alone in that.

There is clearly a reason for it to be well known. It sums up much of the gospel. We could expand the verse to tell anyone who has ears to hear that it was because of God's love that he sent his only Son into world, that the world is lost without a Saviour, but eternal life is promised to all who place their trust in the Son. From that basic statement we can go on to fill out some of the rest of God's gospel plan; that the Son came into the world to save sinners, that he died to take away their sins, that he is the only way of salvation, and that whoever comes to him he will in no wise cast out.

The gospel message is so wonderful that angels desire to look into it! That's a thought, isn't it? The angels in heaven with their much greater knowledge, thousands of years of experience, clearer perception of the glory and majesty of God, find themselves intrigued by the work of God among men and want to know more. We should remind ourselves that it is to fallen men that the privilege is given to praise God particularly for his grace. And what a privilege that is!

All that may mean it is foolhardy for me to take on a verse that is so well known, and loved.

You have probably heard it said that the original word order places the emphasis on the love of God. If it were translated in a rather wooden way it would read, 'So loved God the world ...' Perhaps the very emphasis itself is the greatest weakness. We have become so accustomed to being told that God loves us that we have ceased to wonder at the truth. But there's another handicap from which we suffer: we have such a high opinion of ourselves that we are not surprised that God loves us. I would love me too if I were God! I have even heard sin defined in terms of a lack of self-esteem. That amazes me. Given that virtually all unbelievers, hard-wired as they are for justification by works, believe that their good deeds are sufficient to get them into heaven, the idea that their problem is a lack of self-esteem seems ludicrous to me.

So perhaps the place to start is to ask the question whether God has any reason to love us. We can begin to answer that question by looking at who we love and who loves us. I can think of friends who are very dear to me, and I know quite clearly why I love them. They have shown me kindness in a thousand different ways. Sometimes it may come in the form of a phone call with a few tender and encouraging words. Or it might take the form of a present to mark a birthday. On another occasion it might be a light touch on the shoulder that says more than words. I hope that you can think of those in your circle who have given you so many tokens of their affection that you have long since been past the possibility of numbering them. So have we given God cause to be able to say that this world loves him?

Look at man's record. God made a world that was perfect. It was good not just in man's but in God's estimation. God looked at what he had made and gave his own assessment: 'It was good.' Then what happened? Adam, whom God had appointed as his vice-gerent which is just a fancy way of saying God put Adam in charge, ruined it all. When Adam fell, creation fell with him. (We'll be taking a closer look at this in Meditation 30.)

Now suppose you had made something in which you delighted and then someone came along and ruined it all, would that make you feel a lot of affection towards that person? Of course not.

But perhaps if man had shown himself to be really sorry, that would in some measure make up for what he had done. We are only a few chapters into Genesis when we are told that every intention of the thoughts of man's heart was only evil continually (Gen. 6:5). That doesn't sound much like heart-felt sorrow and repentance, does it? By the time we get to Jeremiah the considered opinion of Scripture is, 'The heart is deceitful above all things, and desperately wicked' (Jer. 17:9 KJV) It's not an attractive picture. When God looks on the heart of man he sees a cesspit of corruption.

The history of the world in every generation is not one of mutual love and understanding with a respect for those less fortunate than oneself. The institutions that we do have often owe their founding to the influences of

Christianity, not to man's innate goodness. Take hospitals for instance. When I was studying at college, I worked as a hospital porter in one of the largest hospitals in the United Kingdom. The nurses in charge of a hospital ward were called 'sisters.' Now why do you suppose they were given that title? It wasn't a nickname. It was their official title. They were called sisters because historically nuns from religious orders ran the institutions that took care of the sick and dying. Care of the sick was one of the reasons why Christianity had such an impact on the Roman Empire in spite of all that the emperors could do to stamp it out.

The cities of the empire were grossly insanitary places, and epidemics would frequently sweep through the cities. The pagan response was to distance oneself from anyone infected no matter how close the relationship. The Christians knowing that 'to live is Christ and to die is gain,' took care of their families and even after their sick and dying pagan neighbours. Such acts of kindness did more than preserve life. They were a tremendous witness to the love of God working in and through his people. But let's not forget its source. Such care for others did not arise out of pagan culture. It was Christians in an early pro-life movement that rescued abandoned babies even when the Senate passed a law against doing so!

So to return to our original question, what reason does God have for loving us? Even the very institutions which most clearly demonstrate care for others, i.e. hospitals, did not arise out of man's own gentleness and kindness but because God had changed hearts.

On the other side, we see much evidence of the cruelty and the wickedness of man's heart of which Jeremiah spoke. If the statistics are accurate, and I have no reason to doubt them, they show us that more people died as a result of war in the twentieth century than in all the previous centuries combined.

What is it that we see when we examine the lives even of our kindly and generous but pagan neighbours? Though it is probably not the best way to introduce the gospel, someone living without Christ has taken all the good gifts God can offer, and has not given him the praise that is his due. How is that really any different from a child taking everything he can from a loving parent and refusing even to say, thank you? (See Meditation 19.)

As we think on this subject we are amazed that God should love us at all. Try as we might, we must come to the conclusion that the reason God loves this fallen rebellious world is hidden in the heart of God. It's certainly not because we deserve it. He gave the altogether lovely one for the altogether unlovable ones. No wonder the apostle John exclaims: 'Behold what manner of love the Father hath bestowed upon us, that we should be called the sons of God' (1 John 3:1 KJV).

But yet there is more for us to see in God's word to amaze and astonish us, for *God is always better than we can imagine*. Take a look at Ephesians 2 again. Paul begins that chapter with a dismal picture of a soul without Christ. We were, he says, following the prince of the power of the air. That's not good company to be in! That is, until God steps in. 'But God …!' No matter how dark the situation, it can be immediately transformed by the power of God.

Now see how Paul goes on to describe this God. He is the one who 'being rich in mercy, because of the great love with which he loved us, even when we were dead in our trespasses, made us alive together with Christ.' Let me give you the rough and rather wooden translation. 'But God, being rich in mercy, on account of his much love with which he loved us, when we were dead in our trespasses, made us alive together in Christ.'

Every time I read those verses of Scripture the enormity of what Paul is saying is impressed on my heart. Sure we can tell our struggling brother or sister in Christ that he or she should take courage because God loves him or her. But Paul is actually bold enough under inspiration of the Holy Spirit to say something more. He tells his readers that they are much loved in heaven.

If this poor struggling heart needs to hear not only that it is loved in heaven, but *much loved in heaven*, then perhaps yours does too.

As you lay your head on the pillow tonight, take this as your comfort: you can say as a child of God that your Father in heaven does more than love you. You are much loved in heaven. Or, as Spurgeon put it, 'He could not love you more, he will not love you less.'

Now, that is good news to fainting hearts.

For further reflection:

1. Who responds to whose love?

2. How does a changed heart change actions?

3. Can you say something more than simply God loves you?

Meditation 29

Thought It Not Robbery—
The Descent from the Throne

Have this mind among yourselves, which is yours
in Christ Jesus, who, though he was in the form
of God, did not count equality with God a thing
to be grasped, but made himself nothing, taking
the form of a servant, being born in the likeness of men. And being found in human form,
he humbled himself by becoming obedient to the
point of death, even death on a cross. Therefore
God has highly exalted him and bestowed on
him the name that is above every name, so that
at the name of Jesus every knee should bow, in
heaven and on earth and under the earth, and
every tongue confess that Jesus Christ is Lord,
to the glory of God the Father.—Philippians 2:5.

A man is strolling along a country lane and his eye lights
upon an ant crossing his path. He stops to watch the ant.
It only seems to know one speed as it rushes along an
invisible path and meets with other ants from its colony,

stopping only long enough for the briefest of exchanges before rushing on. The man continues to observe the ant, and as he does so, he begins to love the ant and the colony from which it came. The more he looks the more he loves the ant. The more he loves the ant, the more he wants to be able to speak to it and make it aware that there is so much more than its small colony of ants, and the invisible path it runs along each day.

It is in that moment that he conceives a plan to become an ant himself, so that he might bring to them all that he desires for them. So the man becomes an ant!

It is just a story. And you may have been thinking that it sounds the most unlikely story you have ever come across. Which is more utterly preposterous? That a man should love an ant, or that a man should want to become an ant? There is a point, of course, to the story. It is meant to illustrate a truth, and as with any illustration it should only be taken on the level of the point it is illustrating. If you press it too far it will fall apart.

Is it strange that a man should love an ant? Yes, it is. They are so dissimilar. In the story the man might just as easily have been strolling along the path and, without even knowing it, crushed the ant underfoot. It is not that he would have struggled to do so. There is besides, only a measurable gap between a man and an ant. The calculation may be immensely difficult to make, and may depend on what elements are included, and the relative weight given to the particular elements, but a man is a finite being, and so is the ant, and therefore the gap in strength, ability and wisdom is a finite one. The gap between the sovereign eternal God and man is infinite. It is only man's colossal pride that stops him from seeing it. But from time to time, and under inspiration of the Holy Spirit, there is a glimpse of reality, as when the Psalmist exclaims, 'What is man that you are mindful of him, the son of man that you care for him?'

When we read in Scripture that 'he humbled himself' that humbling is on a scale that is ultimately beyond our imagination. We have difficulty in comprehending how a man could humble himself to become an ant, or why indeed he would want to do so. How infinitely greater is the gap between God and man, and yet he humbled himself.

Now, if Jesus had been born into the imperial palace in Rome as the son of Caesar, that would have been a humiliation. We sing, perhaps, rather too easily,

> He left his Father's throne above,
> So free, so infinite his love.

So, when did Christ humble himself? In his death? Oh, yes to be sure, but his humiliation began when he entered this world as a man. It is this truth that Paul dwells on in Philippians 2.

The apostle traces Jesus' descent from the throne. Each step in the descent reveals what Jesus set aside, and what he took to himself. He was himself in very nature God. As the Nicene Creed declares, 'very God of very God.' But he did not consider his godhood as something which he needed to grasp as though he might lose it. Instead, he made himself of no reputation. When the citizens of Nazareth brought a plough to be mended by Jesus, they thought they were approaching the son of Joseph not the Son of God.

But there is more. Jesus humbled himself not just to become a man, but to become a servant. The King of kings came to serve. We must look into John's Gospel to recognize what that entailed, for God is always better than we can imagine.

In the good news of Jesus recorded by John, we are told of an evening when Jesus set aside his garments and stooped down to wash the feet of his own disciples. The culture is not our own and the significance will pass us by if we do not know the setting. All those years ago there was no such thing as indoor plumbing or waste disposal units to grind up left overs and rinse them down the drain. Everything you did not want in your house was tossed out into the street. On warm days the smell must have been overpowering. Now, if you were a wealthy person, you might have a dinner party to which you would invite your friends or honoured guests. Those guests, however, would have to pick their way through the rotting vegetation and worse things with which the streets were strewn. When the guests arrived one of the servants of the household would be assigned the task of washing the feet of the guests to remove anything which they might have stepped in on the way to the dinner party. It was the task of the lowest slave in the household. That is the position Jesus adopted with his disciples. He was taking the position of a slave, and not just any slave, but the lowest slave in the household.

How much more can Jesus humble himself? He humbled himself to death. Jesus, the Son of God, through whom all things were made, and without whom nothing was made that was made, the Prince of Life, was obedient unto death.

Like Job we place our hands on our mouths and are reduced to silence by what God has revealed.

But God is always better than we can imagine. We affirm that God came in the flesh and rejoice in God incarnate, but are at a loss to explain how the infinite and eternal can take on himself the likeness of our frail flesh. But Paul goes on to explain that not only did he humble himself in obedience even unto death, but death on a cross.

Have you ever wondered why Jesus had to die that way? If he had to die, could he not have died from old age, or by a sudden accident? Could he not have contracted some illness, slipped into a coma and passed away quietly while in an unconscious state? Why not a catastrophic heart attack? Perfectly fine one moment and gone the next. There are countless ways that a man might die, but Paul tells us explicitly that Jesus humbled himself to death on a cross. It was a judicial death. He died the death of a criminal. No longer fit to walk the earth, and certainly not good enough to enter the heavens, he was suspended between the two: despised and rejected of men.

And more, Jesus was cursed of God. Through endless ages he had enjoyed perfect fellowship with his Father, each loving the other with all the infinite fullness of the Godhead. But on the cross, the Father revealed the fullness of his wrath against all unrighteousness, and out of the love which he has borne towards his people from the foundation of the world, Jesus endured the infinite agony of God's justice. Truly, there never was love like this.

For further reflection:

1. In what did the humiliation of Christ consist?

2. Why did Jesus wash the disciples' feet?

3. Why did Jesus have to die on a cross?

Meditation 30

God's Minimum Wage

> Whatever you do, work heartily, as for the Lord and not for men, knowing that from the Lord you will receive the inheritance as your reward.—Colossians 3:23, 24.

Have you ever called for a plumber and after he has completed whatever repair prompted his visit, found yourself saying, 'No, friend, that is not nearly enough! I insist on paying you more!' That is an experience I have never had, but am eager for the opportunity to enjoy. Just send me his number! I should add that in case there are plumbers reading this, especially those who might be at the end of the line when I need one, I think they are all wonderful fellows who deserve every penny they are paid!

But how much should we pay? Of course that may be the wrong question—I think it probably is. When a person presents his bill, the question is less about what I want to pay and more about what he wants to charge. My choice is restricted to whether I am willing to pay it and when catastrophe approaches my willingness is great.

That is not to say that there is not a place for legitimate discussion, especially when the debate is viewed from the other side. I am keen to pay whatever it takes to avoid a catastrophe—well, *keen* isn't quite the right word but I am at least *willing*. Those at the opposite end of the spectrum find themselves working for rather small amounts, because a crust is better than no bread at all. Such thoughts give rise to questions of whether a society can set a minimum wage. Is it right to set an hourly rate so low that a man cannot provide for himself and his family? Will doing so destroy the very jobs intended to be supported? Well, this is not a book on economics or sustainable commerce, so I am quite prepared to leave the question hanging, and for the consideration of those whose comprehensive grasp of such matters exceeds my own.

What does seem obvious even by raising the question is that a major factor in determining the cost of a person's time is reduced to 'power.' We might be able to dress it up with other academic sounding titles or economic theories but it still comes down to 'the plumber charges what he does because he can.' In that respect those who are the poorest paid are reduced to charging so little for their time, because that is all they can charge. If they had more leverage, then they would charge more. Does the fact that they are unable to charge sufficient to sustain their families mean that they are exploited, or does it mean that were they to charge more they would be out of a job altogether and even worse off? I will leave you to answer that for yourself. My purpose is not to start a debate on economics or politics, but to ask a deeper question than the hourly rate a plumber gets paid.

My question is simply this: has God set a minimum wage? Or to put it crassly, if we were entering into wage negotiations what leverage would we have? What can I offer him that he needs? Of course, our vanity wants us to believe that we are indispensable to his kingdom. If you are tempted by such foolishness, try asking yourself the question, 'Where would God be without me?' If you still don't get the point then perhaps you have never read in your Bible that God said, 'If I were hungry, I wouldn't tell you!' Well, that's you put in your place (and me too)! When Jesus entered into Jerusalem and the authorities wanted him to silence the clamouring crowd he simply responded that if the crowd kept quiet, the stones themselves would have taken up the chorus.

Even with such considerations we are really not grappling with our own position. We are not sitting at the negotiating table as equals. How could we? Even when we have done everything we can do we are only unprofitable servants. 'Everything we can do?' Do we even come close? This is a hypothetical situation to show that even the best of us have no 'leverage.' It is not much of a bargaining position. So, our position boils down to, God does not need anything from us, and whatever we do, can do, or have done is pronounced 'unprofitable.' Was ever an employee's negotiator in a weaker position with an employer? And I have probably over estimated the strength of our position!

I think the prodigal son recognized something of that weakness when he opened negotiations with a wealthy landowner who just happened to be his father. Of course, they had a history. The son had pretty much done everything he could do to make himself odious to his father, and he knew it. His only line left was hoping for some unmerited favour—'Just take me on as a day labourer. The end of the day will be the end of your responsibilities towards me, and I don't even deserve that. When I have done everything you ask me to do, at the end of the day I will still be an unprofitable servant.'

It is not so different from the publican who went up to the temple to pray. He did not come from a strong bargaining position either. Clearly, negotiating was not his strong point. The Pharisee had so much more to offer: praying, tithing, giving to the poor … Just ask anyone! Everyone knew the Pharisee was a generous man. If folks did not know that, they had just plain not been listening. It is not like he hadn't been telling them! But this poor publican gave it all away right from the beginning. He would not even look God in the eye when negotiating. Standing at the back of the temple court he would only beat upon his chest and cry out, 'God be merciful to me a sinner!'

Yet for all the poverty of his plea it was the publican and not the Pharisee who went home 'justified'—God had indeed been merciful to a sinner and forgiven him his sin. That truly is wonderful news as every justified sinner knows. But wait, *God is always better than we can imagine*. We have stood before the judgment seat of God, and the just judge of all the universe has taken the death of his own Son as full payment for our sins against him. We leave the court pronounced not guilty by the only one whose verdict can never be overturned. At that point we might think that life and the blessings of God could not get any better! How could God improve on that?

Well, let me ask you a somewhat unusual question. Have you ever wondered why Jesus was born into the world? I do not mean why he entered the world at all, but why he just didn't wander in from the desert one day to be baptized by John and start his ministry? Would the Gospel records be much different? Some of them would not! Was there any significance to the unrecorded years of childhood, youth and early adulthood. The answer is a resounding, Yes! We can say that our Redeemer not only died for us but he also lived for us. The theologians give fancy titles to this: the death of Jesus was the passive obedience to the will of God to be a sacrifice for sin, the life of Jesus was his active obedience to fulfil the law's demands. The days of Jesus spent in Joseph's carpenter's shop were not obscure—just unknown to us. Each day he lived a life of perfect obedience—the life I ought to have lived, but have not.

The love and grace of God is so staggering that we can hardly find illustrations to convey the truth. William Hendriksen likened it to being before the Judge just as we have pictured, but the Judge not only pronounces us pardoned for the sake of the finished work of Christ, but does so much more. And here is where the illustration becomes difficult to grasp. The Judge goes beyond justifying the sinner, to adopting the sinner into his family and taking him home with him. I expect that judges must see many wretched criminals in the course of a career. How often would he consider adopting a wretch and taking him home with him? Yet,

> The vilest offender who truly believes,
> That moment from Jesus a pardon receives.

So what is God's minimum wage? We will receive the inheritance as our reward. It is not because we have worked so hard or so well that we deserve it—we are after all unprofitable servants. It is not that God has some great need that only we can fulfil. He does not need anything from us. He gives as only God can give, in a way which we can hardly find words to illustrate. For the sake of the life of Jesus he gives of his free grace according to his riches. Yes, he is indeed always better than we can imagine.

For further reflection:

1. What do you have that God needs?

2. How well have you done what God requires of you?

3. What is the reward that God promises you?

Meditation 31

Eye Has Not Seen

Yet among the mature we do impart wisdom, although it is not a wisdom of this age or of the rulers of this age, who are doomed to pass away. But we impart a secret and hidden wisdom of God, which God decreed before the ages for our glory. None of the rulers of this age understood this, for if they had, they would not have crucified the Lord of glory. But, as it is written, 'What no eye has seen, nor ear heard, nor the heart of man imagined, what God has prepared for those who love him'—these things God has revealed to us through the Spirit. For the Spirit searches everything, even the depths of God.

—1 Corinthians 2:6-10.

Congratulations! You are now at the last meditation in this series. It is my prayer that you may have found the past month profitable. I hope that each meditation may have shown you something that perhaps you had not seen before. I am bold enough to hope that it has done something more. I hope that you approach Scripture with a greater expectation. The God we worship is, by definition, *better than we can imagine*, so you and I should always entertain the highest thoughts of him. As Paul said, 'He is able to do exceeding abundantly above all that we ask or think.'

There are three lessons with which I would like to conclude. But first I must deal with one last lingering question: How do we know what to pray for if the answer is exceeding abundantly above all that we ask or think? Surely, logically speaking, we cannot ask for something that is beyond our imagination. Is this a sort of Christian version of asking, what is the sound of one hand clapping?

I think that God in his grace and wisdom has anticipated that question and given us an answer. Paul in writing to the church in Corinth declares that 'What no eye has seen, nor ear heard, nor the heart of man imagined, what God has prepared for those who love him—these things God has revealed to us through the Spirit.'

It certainly is very much in keeping with what we know about a God who is able to do exceeding abundantly above all that we can ask or think. What has God prepared for us—for us who love him? No eye has seen it. So no description then. No ear has heard. So no passing on of information even in the most sanctified lecture. It has not even entered into the heart of man. It is so far beyond man's capacity for rational thought or imagination that it has never, and could never occur to him what God is preparing for those who love him. It is another way of saying 'exceeding abundantly above … [what you can] …

think. We might as well just stop right there and leave it to God. And often I have heard these words quoted and the quotation has ended at that point, if not quite with the shrug of the shoulder, then with little more than a wistful anticipation that no matter how tough life is, our God will bless us greatly in the future. No one knows what that will be like. We can't even imagine it. We just know it will be blissful. Much of that is true. Our future state of blessedness will indeed be much better than our present state, and I am sure it will not in any sense disappoint, but be even better than we can imagine; but that is not the same as saying that we have no idea what it is like at all.

Just take a look at the next verse: 'these things God has revealed to us through the Spirit. For the Spirit searches everything, even the depths of God.' What God is preparing for us may be beyond our imagination, but that is precisely why God can and does reveal these things to us by his Spirit.

Let me use the illustration of a car. My first car was a bit of a clunker. Every so often the link for the accelerator would slip out of place, and I would have to open up the engine compartment and put it back into place. My hopes for the future at that time were really quite simple: a car that had a link to the accelerator that did not break. I have had a number of cars now in the forty years I have been driving, and my expectations have grown. I expect my car to start every time I put the key in the ignition (that was always something of a question in my first car). And then there is air conditioning, and cruise control not to mention cup holders! For the future, I am looking forward to the car that drives itself, and all I have to say is 'Home!' Is that car available now? I do not think so, and if it were, I know I could not afford it. Perhaps my grandchildren, if the Lord should tarry and he should be pleased to grant me any, might retire with such a car. Who knows? I know this: when I first started driving it never entered into my heart that there would be an electronic map on the dashboard of cars, activated by voice, that would tell you how to get to anywhere in the country. It was beyond my imagination. What was beyond my imagination is now a reality. What is now in my imagination I anticipate will one day be a reality.

And that is what God is doing for us through his word. The Spirit is revealing to us God's purposes so that what would not naturally occur to us is taught us from Scripture. Has God not consistently in his word brought us illustration after illustration of the very point that Paul made to the church in Ephesus? That is my thesis: that *God is always better than we can imagine.*

Now there are some implications and applications for us. The first I would have you consider is simply that you cannot exhaust the goodness of God. I will come to what I would suggest you should be asking for in a moment, but let me first encourage you to set aside some less than worthy aspirations.

We live in an age which is obsessed with consumerism. If you do not think so, then ask yourself why divorce is so prevalent. If your spouse is not living up to your expectations, or you would prefer a younger model, just go out and change the one you have. Even the church is just another commodity to be changed when it is not fulfilling one's needs. If you do not like this or that. If the minister wears too loud a tie or his eye brows meet in the middle then just go down the street to another church. In the supermarket of faith you are bound to find the product you like. And you as the consumer have the right to make that choice—or so it would seem judging by how easily folk change churches.

So is prayer just a means by which we can enlist the Almighty to assist us with our own private shopping spree? Well, if we put it like that it sounds rather mercenary. I wish it were an exaggeration. Church then becomes like a visit to grandpa. We like to visit because while we are there we can dip our hands into his pockets and see what loose change he has, and he will not mind if we just scoop it up and place it in our own pockets. We have a generation of churchgoers who are being taught that we should rifle God's pockets for his loose change. It has been a good visit when we come away thinking we have taken a step closer to what we want.

But stop and think about that visit to grandpa. Is it grandpa whom you are delighted to see or is it the contents of his pocket? If he were not there and had left behind the contents of his pockets on the dresser, would it be just as successful a visit? It is heartbreaking to consider how uncomfortably close to the latter we can get. I go to church for what I get from it and not to worship my

Father in heaven. If I do not get anything from it then I am off down the road to another church in the hope that the new church may live up to my expectations. The problem is that we set our hopes on 'that which is not bread.'

And that shows us the absolute folly of sin. We would steal from God what he would so freely give us. Which is better? To have the love of our parents or to have the loose change out of their pockets? What the Spirit reveals through the word is that we cannot exhaust the goodness of God. There never comes a point when he says to us, 'You have used up all my kindness towards you and there is no more.'

There is something further for us to reflect upon and it is this: I do not need to persuade God to do me good. How often do we in our prayers try to haggle with God as though he were a trader in some street market? He has something we want and we enter into negotiation to see how we can get it. 'If you will do this for me, then I will do that for you!' Is that how you negotiate with your parents? Well, perhaps it is, but it is not how it should be. If you are desperately in need and you ask your father for help, and his response is to draw up a contract, then something has gone seriously wrong in the parent-child relationship. So, I say again, we do not need to persuade God to do us good. 'No good thing does he withhold from those who walk uprightly' (Psa. 84:11).

There is one last lesson which we should apply. Perhaps some will remember a speech by President Kennedy at his inauguration: 'Ask not what your country can do for you, but what you can do for your country.' Truly it was a noble sentiment. I think we can borrow it. In a world suffering from terminal consumerism might not our prayer be to love God more? If you pray for the new car your heart desires so much, I cannot guarantee that you will get it. God may or may not grant you what you desire. It may not be for your good. And if it is not, he certainly will not give it to you. But if you pray asking to love him more, he who has told you that you should love him with all your heart soul strength and mind, will grant you what you desire.

So, let this be my last word to you; ask the God of all grace, who is able to do far more abundantly than all that we ask or think, to enlarge your heart to love him more.

> Now to him who is able to do far more abundantly than all that we ask or think, according to the power at work within us, to him be glory in the church and in Christ Jesus throughout all generations, forever and ever. Amen.

About the Publisher

The Banner of Truth Trust originated in 1957 in London. The founders believed that much of the best literature of historic Christianity had been allowed to fall into oblivion and that, under God, its recovery could well lead not only to a strengthening of the church, but to true revival.

Interdenominational in vision, this publishing work is now international, and our lists include a number of contemporary authors, together with classics from the past. The translation of these books into many languages is encouraged.

A monthly magazine, *The Banner of Truth,* is also published and further information about this, and all our other publications, may be found on our website or by contacting either of the offices below.

THE BANNER OF TRUTH TRUST

3 Murrayfield Road
Edinburgh, EH12 6EL
UK

P O Box 621, Carlisle
Pennsylvania 17013
USA

banneroftruth.org